Presented To:

_____

From:

_____

Date:

_____

The
PANORAMIC
SEER

The
PANORAMIC
SEER

Bringing
the
Prophetic
into the
Healing Anointing

JAMES MALONEY

DESTINY IMAGE₀ PUBLISHERS, INC.
P.O. Box 310, Shippensburg, PA 17257-0310
"Promoting Inspired Lives."

This book and all other Destiny Image, Revival Press, MercyPlace, Fresh Bread, Destiny Image Fiction, and Treasure House books are available at Christian bookstores and distributors worldwide.

For a U.S. bookstore nearest you, call 1-800-722-6774.
For more information on foreign distributors, call 717-532-3040.
Reach us on the Internet: www.destinyimage.com.

ISBN 13 TP: 978-0-7684-0302-2
ISBN 13 Ebook: 978-0-7684-8784-8

For Worldwide Distribution, Printed in the U.S.A.
4 5 6 7 8 / 16 15 14 13

DEDICATION

To Joy-Bird, with all my love: my wife, my best friend and my pastor, for nearly four decades of indefatigable support, an anchor, a plumb line for me, rightly dividing the word of truth. If anyone on this planet deserves to hear the applause of heaven… it's you.

ACKNOWLEDGMENTS

Christ for the Nations: the late Gordon and Freda Lindsay, for their pioneering vision and leadership to the body of Christ; Dennis and Ginger Lindsay, for their impartation and grace, furthering the vision of their parents masterfully; all the teaching staff when I attended the Bible college, especially Dr. Carroll Thompson, Dr. Jim Hodges, Joy Dawson, and many, many others, for establishing an unshakeable, liberating foundation in the fear of the Lord, brokenness, contrition, and a servant's heart within the student body.

ENDORSEMENTS

I love this book! It is theology on fire! I need people like James Maloney in my life to show me what is possible by their life and to equip my head, heart and hands for the ministry of Jesus. This book does that for me.

—JIM BAKER, SENIOR PASTOR
Zion Christian Fellowship, Powell, Ohio

Few people I know have the history and experience in the moving of the Holy Spirit as does James Maloney. His personal story is one of my favorites in modern day church history. *The Panoramic Seer* is an invaluable book in this regard: to learn how to recognize and cooperate with the moving of the Holy Spirit as Jesus did. I believe that God will use this to equip hungry believers to live in a realm of the Spirit similar to what God has given to James. I am so happy to see this book finally written. It is an answer to the cry of my own heart for more.

—BILL JOHNSON, SENIOR LEADER
Bethel Church, Redding, California
Author, *When Heaven Invades Earth* & *Essential Guide to Healing*

Dr. Maloney's book, *The Panoramic Seer*, contains powerful revelation and wisdom from God that is so crucial for the Body of Christ. I believe this book is heaven sent for a time such as this where the Body of Christ needs great discernment. Combining his experiential knowledge of God with an in-depth study of the Word of God, Dr. Maloney brings enriching revelation that is sorely needed in the Body today. It is a "Must Read" that you will want to read over and over again as it will equip and edify you.

—RYAN C. LEE, LEAD PASTOR
Blessed International Fellowship, Anaheim, California

James Maloney in *The Panoramic Seer* does a masterful job of presenting scripturally balanced truths that inspire, thrill, and expand our view of the Supernatural Anointing of the Holy Spirit. His vast experience over four decades has given him insight into this subject of ministry through the Power and Gifts of the Holy Spirit that most people never attain. We are blessed to be able to have him share these things with us and benefit greatly by reading this book.

—DR. RONNY D. THOMASON, PASTOR
Cornerstone Church, Jacksonville, Florida

James Maloney is a powerful apostolic father whose ministry has been pivotal to our development as a church. In this inspiring book, *The Panoramic Seer*, James shares many key truths and much timely wisdom that is vital in the current outpouring. Drawing from his broad wisdom and experience of revival, he guides us from the unnecessary pitfalls into the heart of Jesus for the current move of God. He deepens our appetite to walk in the realm of the Spirit, yet gives us firm biblical foundation to work from. This is an essential read for any leader with a passion to see a church flowing in revival.

—PHIL WHITEHEAD, SENIOR PASTOR
Chiswick Christian Centre, London, United Kingdom

CONTENTS

FOREWORD

JOHN THE BELOVED, WHILE ON the Island of Patmos, heard a Voice behind him like the sound of many waters. At the time, he was facing the distant shoreline of Ephesus, 70 miles out beyond the seashore where he was standing. It was Sunday morning, and his precious sons and daughters in the faith in Ephesus, and the other six churches in Asia Minor which were under his bishopric, were gathering to worship the Savior. It was their weekly rhythm to be "in the Spirit" on the Lord's Day.

Mind you, we have the privilege of being "in the Spirit" all the time as joint heirs of Christ, and heirs of the Father. Yet there are those blessed times when the saints gather together and something beyond the one-on-one encounters we have with the Lord get comingled into a confluence of voices in praise and adoration that rise as one voice to the Father of Lights.

So, it was Sunday. Here's John, not in the gathering; rather, he is on a penal colony, sent there by Rome to die in prison. They tried to kill him on other occasions, including boiling him in oil, yet the

Savior's Presence and Power overshadowed him, and even Rome didn't have the ability to take out the Beloved Apostle.

So what did Rome do? They attempted to silence the troublemaker. John's warfare was so intense precisely because of his relationship to The Word of God, the Logos Himself, and the Testimony of Jesus in his life, which by the way IS the spirit of prophecy.

It's rather interesting that they picked the Island of Patmos to banish John to. It's 70 miles out from Asia Minor, a little Greek island on the Aegean Sea. They threw him in a dark, musty cave that when you stared into it, it looked like the abyss, and the end of your own world.

John, however, had turned his face from the dark cave behind him. He made a deliberate decision to turn and face the direction of where the saints were gathering back across the chaotic waters of the Aegean Sea over in Ephesus, that great port city where Paul had pioneered perhaps the greatest expression of the Body of Christ in his entire ministry.

It was the place where Timothy was martyred. It was always a place of intense spiritual warfare that was overcome by intensely passionate worship from the warriors of Christ in that day. When all the other apostles were long gone, and Timothy had been martyred, it fell to John the Beloved, the one promised by Jesus to have longevity, to become Bishop over the works that were in the region.

By this time, John is a seasoned veteran in the Kingdom of Heaven, having fathered 3 generations. Now in this season of transition, when on the verge of crossing the threshold into the 2nd century, the Church for which Christ died is in decline, and they are in danger of reducing Christianity down to a set of rules, having lost the glory of "direct experience" with the Son of God Himself. John the Beloved is the only living witness left who had personal contact with the Son of Man.

No wonder the warfare against him was so fierce. Hell itself could not, with all of its best efforts, extinguish the torch of the testimony in the aging General of Generals, John the Beloved. The old boy still had some "fight" left in him. He still was going to fight the good fight for the sake of an emerging generation that needed to be reintroduced to the Presence and Power of the One Who had so transformed his own life decades ago.

Real fathers in the Kingdom go through REAL WARFARE. I don't think the average believer today fully understands the cost to seasoned warriors who walk in integrity, godly character, and the anointing with power, who have been sustained by the Spirit of God through tribulation and perseverance for the Kingdom's sake; I don't think they realize the price that is paid for the power that is demonstrated in the lives of these great men and women of God.

Suffice it to say, unless you have been there, you cannot comprehend it. One thing I know: John the Beloved had "been there, done that, and bought the t-shirt." One other thing I know: James Maloney has "been there, done that, and bought the t-shirt." Both James and I have had to endure a protracted and strange season we still scratch our heads in mystery over.

Nevertheless, like John the Beloved, when James could have kept his eyes focused in the dark abysmal backdrop of hell's intention to take him out, he made an about-face and deliberately set his sight and his intention on worshipping the Lord. And, like John, he found himself even in his darkest hour, "in the Spirit."

Again, like John, from behind him (doesn't the prophet Isaiah say, "You shall hear a voice behind you..."?), a Voice began to call. Turning in the very direction of the darkest place in his situation, John (and James Maloney) saw the darkness transformed by the Living Presence of the transcendent Christ! There against the backdrop of deep black darkness, standing in royal robes, wearing a glorious crown, holding seven stars in His right hand, stood the Mighty Warrior Himself. The One for Whom it is said, "darkness and light are alike to Thee."

What Rome intended to be an END for John was, in fact, a new beginning, and the birthing place of his greatest days of ministry. For now, John the poet, John the pastor, will begin to speak as John the PROPHET of the DESTINY OF THE BODY OF CHRIST AND OF THE NATIONS!

James Maloney is a seasoned general in the Kingdom of God. I am honored to call him a friend. The work you hold in your hands isn't the by-product of studying notes on any of the major doctrines of Scripture (all of which has its place and benefit; none of which is the same, however, as direct experience with the One about Whom the doctrines speak of).

What you hold in your hands, in fact, is an invitation to a renewed relationship with a living Man; not any Man, mind you, this Man is the Man that is also God the Son! He is the Man in the Glory! One glimpse of Him, and like John, and like James, you will fall at His feet as though you were dead. Yet, He will speak, and immediately His Spirit will revive you, and catch you up into an open door that is standing at the gates of Heaven itself, awaiting your entrance.

There beyond the door, you discover the reality of what those who penned the Apostle's Creed two millennia ago meant when they said, "I believe in the communion of the saints." Call me a mystic, call me a dreamer, call me whatever you will, dead orthodoxy is no match for a living Christ Who upholds all things by the Word of His Power. This living Christ is not the God of the dead, He is the God of the living!

It is unto Him that the gathering of the peoples shall be, in fulfillment of Jacob's prophetic utterance over his son, Judah, so many millennia ago. This One needs to be SEEN, HEARD, FELT, and HANDLED in this new generation if it is to carry the TORCH OF THE TESTIMONY OF JESUS, which is the spirit of prophecy.

James Maloney is inviting you, dear brother and sister, into a very intimate place, where in his transparency, and in his showing you his wounds and his pain, you discover that in the fellowship of the sufferings of Christ, there is also fellowship in the power of His resurrection.

How hungry are you for Him? James, in spite of what he has endured, still has the "fight" in him. And for whose sake is he fighting? As a father in the Kingdom, his warfare and his affliction is for your sake. Don't underestimate what will happen to you as you allow the Holy Spirit to take you on this journey with James.

I assure you, the end result isn't to make you more doctrinally pure, though that will indeed be a result. The end result is for you to have an ongoing, direct experience of intimacy with the One who loved you and gave Himself for you. That, Beloved, is worth the price. And yes, the warfare James endured to bring you these nuggets of truth inspired by the Spirit is priceless as far as Heaven is concerned.

James, I want to thank you for your transparency, and for your willingness to share the powerful kingdom secrets that have sustained the move of God from generation to generation. A great cloud of witnesses who have gone on before us and have fought the good fight and have finished the race surrounds us. They cheer us on and believe for us to finish strong.

Do what James tells you to do, and you will hear them cheering you on, and you too will finish strong!

—DR. MARK CHIRONNA
Mark Chironna Ministries, Orlando, Florida

THEY'RE
WATCHING US

I F YOU'VE EVER WONDERED IF someone in heaven can look down and see us here on earth, in my experience, the answer is yes. At least, as the Lord permits. How I found out that the citizens of heaven can—at times—view us from afar is an interesting story that starts in Manchester, England. I love my friends and colleagues from that city, even if they have ridiculously difficult accents for an American to understand, and are perhaps a little obsessed with their soccer team, but Manchester was a unique place for a life-changing transcendent experience to take place. I wasn't expecting it.

A few years ago I was speaking in a conference with a couple hundred attendees of that fine city. Sitting on the platform during praise and worship, a thought rose up out of my spirit. As I was waiting to be introduced to speak, I asked Jesus a question: Is there any way, Lord, to minister *just like You?* Can that happen by God's grace and wisdom? Can I be so totally yielded to You and Your

Spirit that when I stand up to minister, it would be like *You* were literally standing here ministering instead of me?

Some of you might think that's a presumptuous question to ask God; I mean, who do I think I am, right? But for those of you who know me, I hope that one of the hallmarks of my ministry that I have prayerfully striven for these past four decades is His humbleness established in me. If you know my testimony, you know I shouldn't even be a well-adjusted human, let alone in the ministry. No, I believe it was the Lord orchestrating this thought through me, because when I stood behind the pulpit and opened my mouth to speak, I was awakened to a heightened sense of reality. What I mean by that is, all of a sudden, I entered into a lifting experience where I was caught up in the Spirit. I was aware of my surroundings, I saw the congregation, but it was like I was looking at myself from outside myself, if that makes any sense at all.

We'll get into this a bit more throughout the book, but I felt an anointing *ascend* and rise up out of my spirit-man. At the same time, I felt an anointing from heaven *descend* and merge with mine. It was as if I were cocooned in a complete bubble of God's authority. My spirit's own anointing (from Him initially anyway) was immersed and surrounded by Christ's ministry anointing, and I was "lifted up." That's the best way I can describe it.

I was watching myself teach the Word and preach the message, but I couldn't discern what I was saying. It almost seemed as if my lips moved of their own accord, completely yielded to the Spirit's utterance. I was able to view the people's varying responses and reactions to the message given. Certain aspects of the word were transforming them. There was a "watering" element that was going out to them. They were being fed by the word, and it was producing different reactions. Some were sobbing, weeping, as the word inwardly healed them, turning up and breaking fallow ground, so the watered seed could germinate and bring forth fruit. Some were intoxicated in the Spirit, an oil of gladness filled them to the brim, and their faces shone with the light of the word. Some were studious, listening intently, mixing what they heard with faith, and the revelation transformed their minds. The people were being renewed by the sermon: spirit, soul and body. It was powerful to watch.

I didn't speak very long. Once the sermon was delivered, I stepped down off the platform to move in word of knowledge and prophecy. The prophetic utterances seemed to be extremely specific, and what I want to point out here is how the prophetic itself created an environment for miraculous healings. It appeared that *everyone* was healed. Deformities from birth instantly mended; broken bones snapped into place with audible crackles and pops; tumors disappeared before the people's eyes. All from the prophecies themselves coming forth.

The prophetic mingled and flowed perfectly with words of knowledge, words of wisdom, and destiny was released among the people. Callings and passions were confirmed. Clarity of direction was established. Giftings were quick-started by the spoken word of the Lord. The people burned with new enthusiasm and fervor.

Many people could see the purplish cloud of glory that swirled above our heads, covering over us as I laid hands upon them. Waves of unique fragrances would wash over the crowd, and we would all breathe deeply of some scent of heaven, like fresh flowers and sweet incense. In the distance, many heard a slight crackling, rumbling sound, like rolling thunder moving through the congregation.

When someone fell under the power of the Spirit, I didn't even have to touch them. They would collapse, trance-like, into a deep, abiding realm. They stayed down, some for lengthy periods of time, while a profound work of cleansing and renewing was accomplished. When they came to, they seemed absolutely altered in their spirits and bodies, unaware of their surroundings and helped back to their seats so they could just worship the Lord.

Everything was happening that the people needed; none was neglected or untouched that I saw. And the Spirit was moving everywhere, simultaneously touching this one, healing another, speaking to another, all at once. Yet, everything was done decently in order, orchestrated flawlessly and effortlessly. What was so refreshing was that the ministry was very easy and relaxed; it was all so *simple*, but not trite. The intensity of the ministry was such that, at times, hushed reverence would fall over portions of the crowd. Some fell on their faces and wept, prostrate before the Lord. At other times, some rejoiced loudly, exuberantly celebrating the works of God. Yet through all that intensity, it was executed in an atmosphere of restfulness and liberty. It was enjoyable and fun!

About an hour and a half later, I felt the work was completed. Nothing else needed to be done. As I stepped back onto the platform, I felt a separation of the anointing. Descending into my spirit-man, ascending up to the Lord. I was "inside" myself once again, and my heart cried out in desperation for that zeal of the Lord to consume me. Did it work? Did I do it right? Oh, Lord Jesus, did I do it correctly? Was it just like You would've done?

Immediately I was caught up to heaven. Now, just like Paul in 2 Corinthians 12, I'm not sure if my spirit left my body and was taken to heaven, or if it was like a movie screen outside my mind that opened up, or what. I don't know which. All I can say is I did not "see" this in my brain—it was outside my mind's eye. I saw this externally with my real eyes.

Somehow, as I was instantly in heaven, I just knew the room I was standing in was directly adjacent to the throne room of the Father. I didn't see the throne room, but this antechamber alone was enough to make my jaw drop open. Twelve circular pillars surrounded the room on two sides, twenty-four total. These pillars were ornately carved and etched beyond any meager human description. The pillars alone were beauty manifested; nothing can be compared to them, encrusted with the richest, largest jewels and gemstones—they were spectacular!

Then I looked down to where I was standing, and the floor blew me away. It was see-through. The scripture in Revelation 15 came to my mind. I was looking on a sea of glass mingled with fire. It's hard to describe. The floor was clear as crystal with a slight bluish hue, but under the glass were crackling flames of fire mixed all through it. And you could see down on earth, like watching a television, but almost like you were right *there*.

Then I noticed the people. Don't know how I could've missed them. *Um, hey, how's it going?*

Somehow I knew there were one thousand saints of God sitting on the floor, looking down through the sea of glass, and they were viewing the service I was just at. They were permitted to watch me preach and minister. It's an odd notion, watching them watching you down there while you're up here, watching them watching you. I've confused myself...

I glanced quickly at some of their faces, and I recognized two or three of them. These individuals were instrumental in the first few years of my spiritual development, great sisters and brothers who encouraged my faith and helped teach me sensitivity to the Spirit's promptings.

Feeling that prompting, I asked the question again. Was I yielded to You, Jesus, so much so that it was as if You Yourself were ministering to the people? *Did I do it right?*

Immediately when I asked, all the people in the Viewing Room stood to their feet and faced me. They looked at me for a few seconds, and then—they applauded...

After this occurrence, the Spirit revealed five keys to me. Five simple notions that help get each of us in a place of submission to the Lord where He moves through us as if He were ministering, not us. If you read my autobiography, you know I don't believe experiences like this are just for one man or one woman only. I believe there are principles we can extrapolate from an encounter like this to be applied in every believer's life. So after they applauded, I asked, what can I take from this to help instruct others?

Firstly, I believe the Spirit revealed an attribute of *inheritance* in the anointing. The development of the anointing can start from a "download" of the previous generation. In my case, my connection to the Golden Candlestick ministry. Frances Metcalfe's seer operation, at least after a fashion, was translated into my ministry. I believe an element of the anointing can be transferred, and we will discuss some concepts of this transference.

Secondly, there is a key of *righteousness* in the anointing. It is directly tied to your comprehension of your right-standing with God, and His demand for holiness in your life. We will outline and dissect some doctrinal truths regarding this component.

Next, *compassion* plays a vital role in ministering as Jesus did. It isn't just *your* compassion for the lost and hurting. It is a supernatural mixing with *His* compassion that permits His anointing to flow through you.

Faith in the anointing cannot be emphasized enough. But I don't mean just *your* faith toward Him alone—it takes a gift of faith, a divine instilling of the Lord's faith in Himself to operate as He did. I am persuaded it is next to an impossibility for any individual person's own faith to be deepened enough to see creative miracles take place (i.e., toes to grow instantly where none existed a moment before, *those* kinds of miracles). It is my experience that there is always a supernatural degree of His faith imparted the moment a miracle like that occurs. We'll discuss this idea more fully.

Lastly, and perhaps most importantly, I think one of the single greatest factors in the anointing stems from *humility*. Coming to the revelation that you have absolutely nothing in yourself to be able to minister to people, apart from your direct revelation and relationship with the Lord. We must be trained to allow the Lord to minister through us. We must decrease, and He must increase (see John 3:30). The question is, how do we do that? We'll take a look at this concept first.

We will tie all this into an element of the prophetic, since I believe the supernatural goes hand in hand with it, and I hope to provide some intriguing illustrations to highlight what we're talking about. We'll discuss the seer anointing, and how it ties into panorama, which I'll give a bit better definition for in the following chapters. Actually we'll look a little bit at anointing in general.

We'll also take a look at some of the characteristics required to develop this type of operation, to thicken the anointing, as it were; what God is looking for when those watching give their applause. It's not just the manifestation, it's the fruit *behind* the manifestation.

I pray this book will be a blessing; I trust in the Spirit that He will bear witness to you of the concepts presented in these pages, subjected to the entire council of the written Word of God; but lastly, I pray this book to be a catalyst for your ministry expression, at whatever level it may be—I pray there are truths contained in this book that will benefit everyone's relationship with the Lord in some way. And by God's grace, with His anointing and instruction within us, we can allow Him to move through us in such a way that we all hear the applause of heaven.

ADRENAL FATIGUE

L ET ME TELL YOU, NERVOUS exhaustion breakdowns are no fun! Anyone out there reading this who's had one knows exactly what I'm talking about. You can't catch your breath, you sweat profusely, you think you're losing your mind. After a fashion, that's probably pretty accurate. There's a sense of desperation, that you won't recover, that you need to climb the walls, but you're too tired to even move. Panic! You want to lay on the floor and curl up like a baby. You wanna be sedated just to get through it. I'm not being facetious here.

After more than thirty-five years of full-time itinerant ministry, averaging three hundred services a year, seventy some-odd overseas crusades to places like the jungles of India, the civil wars of Mozambique and the deserts of Yemen—in October, 2009, my body just shut down. That's it, stick a fork in me, I'm done. The doctors called it "severe adrenal fatigue." Emphasis on the word "severe."

One's adrenal glands sit atop the kidneys and are vitally important for regulating stress levels, among other things. My adrenal glands just took a vacation; no more adrenaline for you, James Maloney! The hormone levels in my endocrine system got all out of whack. And your body requires cortisol and adrenaline to function properly, even to survive. Adrenaline is just one of those things that people need, you know, like… air. Kind of important…

I couldn't sleep, the walls were closing in on me, suffocating; my skin crawled with a million ants; my hands wouldn't stop shaking, and my face twitched.

I was a mess. And I was a healing evangelist. How'd that happen, right?

Like so many ministers out there, I was always pressing, always going, always on the move. Gotta go, go, go! The world is hurting, and Jesus is coming. Get busy! I felt that in each of my meetings, I was failing the people if I didn't give 110 percent.

There's nothing wrong in ministering this way, provided we all follow the natural laws that God created requiring the human body to rest and recuperate. It is honorable and productive to have a sense of urgency and drive in one's life. But how many of us know of powerful evangelists and preachers, bright stars glowing white-hot that burn out too quickly? The Lord showed me another way. It was not His will, nor His desire, for me to face this physical attack. It was my own fault, but in His infinite grace and wisdom, He turned a situation that in the natural would most likely have thwarted my public ministry into an occasion for testimony.

Some of my friends and colleagues have also faced adrenal fatigue. Many of them required hospitalization. Thankfully, the Lord spared me from such, but there were times I was very, very close to having my wife take me to the emergency room. The doctors told me that adrenal fatigue takes at least two years to recover from, and that I should get out of the ministry. If I pushed it, the damage could be permanent.

But I rejected that and went back to traveling two months later, albeit at a greatly reduced pace. After being used to three weekends a month travelling, minimum, and often several weekends back-to-back, I now was forced to go out every other weekend. I would minister at night, crawl into bed, and get up just in time for the next service the following evening. It was that bad. Often I would be bodily carried out of the services, placed into the car, and driven back to the hotel room. Most of the time, I simply sat on a stool in front of the congregation and taught.

I believe it was the grace of the Lord that permitted me to minister at all, since it is my family's source of income. The Lord began hastening the recovery process, but I was by no means "well." Every time I stood up to preach, I'd feel a wave of panic break over me. What if I lapsed back into those symptoms again? What if next time was worse? It's possible for adrenal fatigue to lead to strokes. Now, as a faith minister, I knew the Lord was protecting me, but that doesn't mean the circumstances go away, and that doesn't mean one should be foolishly presumptuous with that protection!

I called my wife after a particularly bad attack, thinking I had rushed back into full-time ministry too quickly. She told me she'd had a dream. Now, for those of you who know my wife, you know when she has a dream, folks better listen. When people ask who my pastor is, I without hesitation reply, "Joy Maloney."

"Jim," (she can call me Jim; I prefer everyone else to call me James) "Jim," she said, "I had a dream. I saw a generator on the ground, and it was broken. The generator is the way you used to do things, operating often out of your own strength and personal anointing. After so many years of ministering, you'd gotten comfortable in the way you moved in your gifts. You relied on your own way of teaching and preaching and ministering. That's not wrong, but there is an end to that. Your personal generator is broken, and the Lord says He's not going to fix it. It will stay broken, so that you will learn to rely utterly on Him, like you did in the early days of your ministry. Then I saw two power cables descend out of heaven, and a thundering voice said you would have to learn to grasp onto the power cables from heaven to continue ministering, so that the anointing would come directly from Him."

Now, my friends, how many know that's a pretty specific dream, and a very humbling one at the same time? I had to relearn my reliance upon the Lord's grace; I had to enter into His rest, and from out of that, the ministry He had entrusted to me could continue, to go deeper. But it stemmed from a reprogramming of my brain, similar to how my adrenal glands had to "reboot" and start over again.

Now before everyone gets bent all out of shape because I'm about to talk about angel manifestations, please keep this understanding in the front of your mind (and for those who've read my previous books, you'll know this already): I do *not* place an overemphasis on the angelic. While I most certainly honor their ministry to us and the Lord, for that is what an angel does, I emphasize the importance of recognizing they are simply co-laborers with us. We have a tendency, I believe, in glory-circles to get a little carried away with angels, and I have seen some groups border on angel worship, sad to say. But on the other side of the coin, some groups have a tendency to get a little carried away pooh-poohing the angelic activity, and it stunts them. So please recognize there is a balance here that needs to be learned: we do not shun the angelic, nor do we place them on some sort of pedestal. They are what they are. I do not advocate "angel contact" or summoning the heavenly host, any of that. This is one of the sovereign things that if the Lord deems proper, they will manifest; if they do not, no worries, move along. However, I do think it is proper for us to be in a position with the Lord (again, through the secret place, out of relationship with *Him*) that, if He so chooses, the angelic is bodily welcome in our midst.

Bottom line is, whether we want to admit it or not, the angelic is constantly in motion, between this world and the third heaven, ministering to us and unto the Lord, responding to our intercession, giving direction and utterance as the Lord wills, hampering the demonic in works of deliverance, executing the judgments of God, so on and so forth.

They can (but not always) be messengers of healing. I do not really believe there is *just* a healing angel, in that strictest sense. Or a prophetic angel. Or a warring angel who is nothing else but a warrior, or a judgment angel that is nothing else but a judgment angel. I think that's probably correct; though I guess there could be an angel that is nothing else but a specific type. I suppose we cannot be completely doctrinal about it one way or the other; it's just my opinion.

In any case, I believe there are angels in general, and they are assigned to various tasks; but note, I'm not saying there aren't levels of angels: archangels, seraphim, cherubim, etc. I simply mean sometimes we teach that there's a specific angel for each manifestation or grace or act of God, and I'm not convinced that is always the case. Nor will I argue about angel gender. It is my opinion they're not really either or, but appear as they want, and could appear male or female as needed, whether or not specific chapter and verse exists. I have seen them as shafts of flame, extremely tall, averaged size, with wings, without wings, in normal clothes, in heavenly armor, all different colors of skin and hair.

I think they are able to change their appearance, just as Lucifer can transform into an angel of light at his whim (see 2 Corinthians 11:14). I can assure you, out of my own experience, that is the case: Paul is speaking literally about Lucifer's capability to metamorphose into something other than what he is. Not all demons appear ugly.

That's beside the point. What needs to be said concerning the ministry of the angelic is they can bring a strengthening to our own ministrations. While I wholly agree with biblical teaching on general angelic involvement in the gathering of the saints' prayers (see Revelation 8:4) and their role in responding to intercession; and while pretty much every Christian believes there are angels for war; and while we see in scripture that they are instruments of God's judgment, I am convinced by experience they can be assigned to a specific task, given a specific anointing, and given to a specific person for a specific need. That's pretty specific, you know? It's not some intangible, floaty "force" or energy, but a real being with a real task that strengthens a person like you or me in a time of need.

At least such has been the case with my operation in panorama. It has been the same angel for almost forty years (and probably a few more, God willing.) No, I don't know his name; no, I don't have conversations with him; no, I don't see him every time I turn on a light switch. I could not describe him in detail to you. He descends at the time of ministry, and then ascends when it is over. (I say "him" because the times I have seen him, he appears male, but again I am not being adamant on gender. I don't believe he is a "he" or a "she"—but it is insulting to call him an "it.")

So with all of that as a preface, let me share what happened after the adrenal fatigue, when I was speaking at a conference on releasing the mechanics of the healing anointing (we'll define that in a little bit) in St. Paul/Minneapolis. I guess a few hundred people were in attendance, a lot of the Healing Room directors and many folks coming in for the event from elsewhere. A lot of healing needs were present at the gathering.

After my physical condition, I remember thinking I wouldn't even be able to walk up to the platform, let alone minister to anyone. It took every bit of strength I possessed to bumble through a twenty or thirty minute teaching, and afterward I was utterly exhausted. During the whole grueling ordeal, I kept telling the Spirit, "I can't do this. I can't minister to anyone. I'm just going to have them take me back to the hotel."

But I felt the prompting of the Spirit, specifically toward a Hispanic lady that I felt impressed upon to minister to. I kept brushing off the nudge. "I'm too exhausted, Lord. I have no strength for this." Initially the prompting was a real sweet wooing of the Holy Spirit, a flow of love (we'll discuss this later, too) toward this person. "Call her up, I want to minister to her," I kept feeling. Maybe four or five times during the course of the message, "Call her up," and then as I finished my teaching, the impression became more emphatic, as if the Holy Spirit was starting to get perturbed at my fighting with Him about calling up the woman.

Finally the Spirit became stern. "Call her up *now*."

I sighed and gave in, stubborn man that I am. Like some limp dishrag, I asked for her to come forward, and I felt impressed upon that she should come stand by my right side.

Now, a little aside here: I have always felt that the discerning of spirits operation (again, more on this later—hang in there!) originates in my right hand. This started in fall of 1975, but through the years, I've come to recognize it better, and the Lord has deepened the operation. I talked a little bit about this in *The Dancing Hand of God*, so don't think I'm making this up on the fly. The manifestation I feel in this kind of operation is not only coming up from my spirit-man in an internal, intuitive fashion, but outwardly in the realm of physical sensations that are deposited in the palm of my right hand, so that I am aware of the Spirit's moving.

I want to stress it's not so much a healing anointing or a workings of miracles, but rather that when I lay my hand upon a person, I can sense—I hate to use the word "detect;" it's a little frou-frou, but it's a good description—what the Father wants to do for the person, in the name of healing or deliverance, etc. Specifically, especially as the panoramic operation becomes more condensed and focused, it is a tool the Lord permits me to use for sensing if a spirit of infirmity plagues the person or not. It's like a lump of burning coal in the center of my palm that goes into the person, and I am aware if their infirmity or weakness is demonic or not. Sometimes I will sense the movings of the Spirit in my fingertips that, after a while, I've learned to discern mean a certain type of healing, or a certain type of infirmity, is present.

If it is a spirit of infirmity, we take authority over it, it is cast out, and then the hindrance is removed for the Lord to work a healing or miracle as needed. In the case of a creative or recreative miracle, the heat in my palm will continue, getting more intense, and I know that the workings of miracles is taking place. (A recreative miracle means when something used to work right and doesn't any longer, like an arm that was crushed and never mended properly. It needs to be *recreated*. A creative miracle is when something never worked right in the first place. Like a person born deaf whose ear drum was never *created*.)

Very handy, this discernment operation is, of which I am most humbled and thankful to the Lord that He is gracious enough to operate in this way for the person's benefit, and my own as well.

So obviously it would make sense that I felt impressed to have the lady at the Minnesota conference approach my right side. I took her hand into my right hand, mostly so that I wouldn't fall, I was so fatigued—but also, as I took her hand, I had the physical sensation of a person bumping into my right side. What was incredible to me, was I felt his elbow rest on my right shoulder so that his arm extended over mine. Think about that. I'm six-foot-five, so this angel must be pretty tall to reach over my arm.

I heard the Holy Spirit speak. What I mean by that is, it was audible in my ears, not just an internal voice—but I don't believe others heard Him. He said, "Enter into the strength of the angel I have sent you."

Immediately I saw the flash of a very intense, swirling golden flame-like cloud envelop the sister and me—as thick as it was round; I mean, solid, not a hollow tube. For those who read my first book, you'll recall the pillar vision—that was this flaming cloud. And I instantly felt superhuman—I joke that I "changed clothes in a phone booth," like Superman. All fatigue and tiredness evaporated, and a rush of the Lord's strength whooshed through me. The discernment of spirits operation began working in my hand like it had before, but I felt compelled to look up.

As my eyes focused just above her head, to my left and right I saw snapshots come out of my thoughts and begin to move. I mean, these were not open visions; they were thoughts from my own brain and spirit, an inner vision, but it's like they came out of my mind and were displayed before my open eyes—I could still see the walls and the ceiling of the auditorium, but it's like these thought-pictures were superimposed over my natural surroundings. They began as still photographs, but parts of the photographs started to have motion. The word "seven" flashed through these snapshots.

"Well," I began, "I see, like, seven years ago you were in a car wreck, someone hit you in a red pickup truck. Is that right?"

"Yes," the lady said.

The snapshots moved again. "And you had to have hip replacement surgery. Is that correct?"

"Uh-huh."

Then I described vertebra that were cracked, and over the course of about ten minutes, I described five or six different things that were wrong with her. It was easy because I was just describing the pictures I saw above her head. The lady was sobbing and weeping, and everyone was shocked by what was transpiring, myself more than any of them. What was great was that each thing I described, she was getting healed of. You could hear *snap, crackle, pop* as bones mended. I was told later that there was titanium in her hip that dissolved. All those things I described wrong with her were recreated, and she proclaimed that the descriptions I gave were one hundred percent accurate.

After I was done ministering to her, I felt this glory cloud lift and the most intense emptying of strength I've ever encountered in any kind of ministry. Panoramic operation like this is the most draining thing, but over the last year or so, I've been able to build up enough strength to move in usually three or four of this type of operation. I think I've done as much as eight or nine at one time, but that's rare.

An interesting facet to these kinds of panorama is I sense a downloading of the gift of God's faith. It's supernatural to have the confidence to know that you know that you know the specifics you're sharing are from God. There's no way in the natural I could be bold enough to explain what I was seeing without a level of the God-kind of faith being imparted at the time I start seeing the revelations.

While in this kind of operation, it's very exciting and addictive. You love having that kind of faith and divine strength, but it leaves you wiped out when it lifts. Still, this gift of faith starts spilling out into the congregation as they listen to what's being said. People know that I know nothing about these people I'm ministering to, and such specifics are being revealed that it supercharges their own faith to receive.

There's not so much of a reactionary response to the operation—not much exuberant praise and rejoicing. Most often, the people sob and weep in awe-filled reverence. It's such a humbling experience.

I don't do this every time, but if I feel led, what I'll do is have the people start praying in tongues, and I'll move up and down the aisles. Under this operation, I am able by God's grace to discern their prayers (tongues and interpretation of tongues, see 1 Corinthians 12-14), and the thoughts and intents of their hearts are revealed. So I get snapshots of the three, four, five I'm supposed to call out—that doesn't mean God loves those people more; it's just a sign and wonder that increases the corporate level of faith.

Of course, some of the people can only pray in English, and it works for them as well; and some of them aren't even saved that are called out—it's not just for the saints. This panoramic operation is a wonderful, evangelistic tool that I feel is going to be used to bring in the lost. Primarily, for right now, it is geared mainly for the church, although we have seen many unsaved people respond to the operation; but in the years to come, I believe this kind of move is really going to be used as a sign and wonder to bring the disbelieving into the kingdom.

As this gift of faith goes out to the congregation, I have found that the more the people pull on the operation, the greater the expression of it becomes. What I mean is that as the people pull upon the anointing in faith, rather than just sit idly as spectators, the Lord responds to their desire. There is a real connection between the people's yearning to see the manifestation of God's presence and the level of clarity of panoramic operation that the Lord permits me to utilize. It's an amazing correlation to experience. It creates an involvement for the corporate body, more so than just an individual gift the Spirit allows me to operate in.

Yes, I believe this type of operation really came to the forefront once I was unable to minister in my own strength. The Lord knew that if He didn't support my flagging vigor, my public ministry was over. But the people themselves play just as much, if not more, of a significant role than myself.

To a certain extent, I have always moved in a seer operation with panoramic expression since getting into the ministry, even if I didn't know what to call it or the doctrinal teaching behind it. So it's not something entirely new. But since my adrenals crashed, the Lord told me it would be an intense, concentrated, *focused* anointing that would come forth as I rested in the strength of the ministering angel He sent alongside to help. He told me to be still, silent, to wait upon Him, and from that would flow this distilled operation.

Generally this panorama is for the purpose of releasing the miraculous or the healing anointing, but I'm starting to learn now, if I don't sense a particular night is for healing or miracles, that the Lord is gracious enough even to permit this panorama to enhance personal prophetic words over people coupled with a real sense of refreshing for the congregation. It's very versatile.

Since I'm not 100 percent restored in my adrenal glands, I usually can only operate in panorama with four or five people— but since that gift of faith extends to the people, it's like they're brought up to that level of the God-kind of faith where their own expectations are answered by the Lord. So I just pull up a stool and stand in agreement with the people for whatever they're in need of. That discernment of spirits operation is still in effect, and I can just work *with* them, speaking over them, sometimes asking them to activate their faith by doing something they couldn't do without being healed. That's the nature of workings of miracles—working the miracle out in faith. It's fun and powerful to watch God move like that.

I'm not sure why, but often it's in this kind of flow that we see some of the most dynamic miracles to God's glory and honor alone, as if the panorama increased the subsequent ministry ten-fold. Blind eyes cleared; deaf ears opened; crooked bones made straight; tumors dissolved; debilitating conditions reversed; great signs and wonders produced, especially in the realm of metal disappearing out of people's bodies. That's a rush! Often there's a rancid, acrid smell, and the metal comes out of people's pores. Sometimes there are voluminous amounts, covering the carpet with metal flakes or drops. Now if that doesn't get you shouting and worshiping the Lord, you're already comatose.

Here's a bunny trail, but I get asked this a lot, so I'll address it here: I don't know why sometimes the metal dematerializes, and sometimes God changes the composition of the metal to mimic bone or tissue or whatever. Like, some people will go get an X-ray, and the rod in their back will be there still, but it moves identically with the bone, just as flexible. I know it's strange, but I don't have an answer for it. His choice, not mine, and in some ways I think that's probably a greater sign and wonder than if the metal just disappeared.

What's the coolest thing is we get e-mails from pastors sharing the residual effect upon the congregation: continued signs and wonders, greater healings and manifestations of His presence, salvations and deliverances, a corporate identity of the people reproducing the panoramic release. How tremendous is that! It's like a catalyst for inciting the people into replicating similar manifestations of His glory that God is bringing us into in these end-times. That to me is the greatest thing about panorama.

So that's how this book came about, and now we can move on into the meat of it. I want to deepen this panoramic operation, but I also have to remember that the old way of doing things has ended. While I am recovering from the physical effects of the adrenal fatigue, the Lord has made it clear that my continued ministry is from an utter reliance on His strength and grace. In a way, I had to unlearn what I had learned during the past thirty-five years of ministry. I had to relearn a reliance upon the anointing.

SMEARED

HERE'S AS GOOD A PLACE as any to diverge for a moment to talk about anointing. In the Hebrew, the word *mashach* (Strong's # 4886) means "to rub or smear (with oil)." The Greek equivalent is *chrio* (Strong's #5548), which should bring to mind Christ, the "anointed One," and by association, Christian, "a little anointed one." To be Christian is to be "anointed" by the very context of the word.

What is the anointing for? In the broadest sense, it is to uplift the people, to raise them up, to elevate them into the presence of the Lord. More specifically, the anointing is to remove pain and hurt off the people so that they are in a place to receive from God. In essence, the anointing oil is a painkiller for all the external and internal wounds of a person.

The anointing oil of Exodus 30 is a natural representation of the spiritual anointing oil, that is, the Holy Spirit. It was comprised of five ingredients, each representative of a spiritual connection.

Myrrh is a sticky, gummy substance that is still used as a pain deadener. It represents a mixture of love and suffering, compassion and passion, what moves you to care on the behalf of another, and what you are willing to suffer for.

Cinnamon is a highly flammable spice, representative of spiritual "fire"—revival—glowing, burning jealously for the honor of God, great zeal that quickly catches light and burns uncontrollably.

Calamus is also called Sweet Flag, a cane-type plant that grows among water lilies, and it is known for aromatic properties, when it is bruised or crushed (that's important to remember for the following couple chapters). It represents forgiveness from betrayals and woundings. As we are pressed and crushed, we can choose to become rancid, or allow the treasure within to come forth with a pleasant aroma. The crushings of ministry are often bittersweet; it is our decisions that affect the smell of our service toward others.

The plant grows straight up and out of miry streambeds, implying we, too, should stand up right in the midst of sin and perversion. As an interesting aside that comes free with the cover price of the book, calamus keeps insects away; it is also believed to counteract the effects of hallucinogens—it clears the mind of clutter; and it is known to help with flatulence—give me a minute and I can tie that into something spiritual…

Moving right along.

Cassia is bark scraped from a tree. It represents sacrifice, worship, brokenness, sharing the concept of stooping over in order to serve the people we are ministering to. It is the purity element of the anointing oil. Cassia must be scraped off, split from the tree, and shows the purging element of the Holy Spirit. For the holy anointing oil is only given by the Holy Spirit to a holy priesthood. That's a lot of "holy."

Lastly, is olive oil: the ingredient added by which the aroma of the anointing oil is enhanced, made pungent to the nostrils. It represents the power of the Holy Spirit and the manifestation of His presence to mankind. It holds the mixture together.

Now like I highlighted in the experience in the previous chapter, each of us has our own *personal* anointing (what ascends up from our spirit-man) and out to the people. Primarily, this is what we are anointed *to be* (an appointment). It is our relationship with Christ, brought about by the Holy Spirit. How we are able to relate to God personally, to understand His ways, to receive and hear from Him. This is represented in the Greek word *chrisma* (Strong's #5545; see 1 John 2:27 as one example), not to be confused with *charisma* (Strong's #5486).

This personal anointing is everlasting, a fountain of living water than never diminishes, but it doesn't really "grow" in strength, in the strictest sense—I mean, our relationship with Christ grows, but the *ability* to have that relationship does not. One either has it, or one does not. We are anointed in this manner in the baptism of the Holy Ghost into Jesus Christ (what is theologically termed "baptized unto Christ" at salvation and the subsequent "baptism into the Holy Spirit" with the evidence of speaking in tongues). This is for our individual walk with the Lord.

Now, out of this anointing we can bless people, but since it is "limited," in a sense, we cannot *completely* convey the anointing, or glory of God, to others.

But there is a greater, deeper anointing in the baptism in the Holy Spirit that is Christ's, which descends upon us, and mingles with our own. We call this the *ministerial* anointing. It is what we are anointed *to do* (a proclamation). A special touch for a special task. This type of anointing is provisional and "lifts off" after the ministry is complete.

Now, keep in mind, *all* anointing, personal and ministerial, is only Christ's anointing; in ourselves, we have no anointing apart from what He entrusts to us. If we attempt to access anointing in ourselves, apart from delegated authority, it is embezzled and leads to defilement. (See *The Dancing Hand of God* for more information.)

"For in Him dwells all the fullness of the Godhead bodily; and you are complete in Him, who is the head of all principality and power." (Colossians 2:9-10)

To be completed in Him is to be covered over, cocooned and bubbled in His fullness: the essence of the Godhead bodily contained in Jesus Christ, the source of all power, mingling and completing your own level of grace-gifting.

It is from His ascension, in His glorified body, that the limitless ability of His anointing is contained. It is melded with humanity, because He wanted it that way: Jesus being the head or origination, we being the representative body on this earth. This is the anointing of Christ descending upon us, and we are made complete in representation of His authority and force, when we are yielded to Him. Yet because of His desire and passion to co-labor with us, He has shared, or given through delegated authority, a portion of anointing personally to call our own. Thus, with the completeness of Christ, we can operate just as if Christ Himself was ministering.

The anointing breaks yokes of bondage (weights) off the people (see Isaiah 10:27). It is the Holy Spirit's active working to implement any particular victory won by the cross, purchased by the blood of Jesus. It is the authority (*exousia*, Strong's #1849) and power (*dunamis*, Strong's #1411) that is delegated to the followers of Christ. Reference Luke 9:1 as just one example. A key to note is the anointing can be transferred through impartation and out of relationship.

We seem to think that the anointing is *only* given sovereignly by God, and while it is certainly true that many of God's anointed ministers were solely commissioned by Him, there is a principle in understanding that the anointing can be transferred from one to another, at least in a measure. Of course, the anointing is not just given on a whim, for it must be guarded zealously, but it comes out of affiliation with established ministers, being knit together in unity, and imparted from one generation to the next—like Moses to Joshua, Elijah to Elisha, Jesus to His disciples, Paul to Timothy, and so on.

The anointing brings insight (see Revelation 3:18); gives authority (see 2 Samuel 5:3-4); it can bring material blessing (Numbers 18:8); establish effective ministry (Luke 4:18; Acts 10:30); it is the power for victorious living (2 Corinthians 1:20-22); and the means of knowing truth (see 1 John 2:20-21). It is vital to the ministry of the believer, but it must be cultivated.

The anointing releases us from intimidation, making us bold to minister as Jesus ministered, thus meriting the applause of heaven. But we must learn to be wholly centered on the Lord (not the circumstances we are believing to change or the person we are ministering to), for no matter what, it is all *His* anointing, power and authority; and it is *Him* who ministers, with us being an empty conduit for His power to flow through.

Let's discuss the healing anointing for a bit. This is another facet of the anointing, specifically for breaking the yokes of sickness and disease off the people. The vast majority of our ministry to the world is in the realm of healing, since that is what most people, saved and unsaved, are in need of. Healing is an expression of God's love to the lost, wooing them to come into the kingdom. Healing is an expression of God's love to His people, as it is their right to make a demand on His anointing for physical well-being. In fact, the premise of the healing anointing is to bring about divine *health*—a state of healthful existence, the absence of life-threatening disease and major illness, to the point of reaching zero sickness, no matter how minor. That's the plan for His children, but until we reach that point—it is our right to be able to call upon the Lord for our healing needs.

Jesus is our great example of resident healing anointing.

> *"Then Jesus returned in the power of the Spirit to Galilee, and news of Him went out through all the surrounding region... And He was handed the book of the prophet Isaiah. And when He had opened the book, He found the place where it was written: 'The Spirit of the Lord is upon Me, because He has anointed Me to preach the gospel to the poor; He has sent Me to heal the brokenhearted, to proclaim liberty to the captives and recovery of sight to the blind, to set at liberty those who are oppressed; to proclaim the acceptable year of the Lord.'"* (Luke 4:14, 17-19)

After His testing in the wilderness, note that Jesus "returned in the power of the Spirit." Prior to His returning in power, we see in Verse 1, He was previously filled with the Spirit—showing a progression: being filled with the Spirit, being tested and tried, and then being anointed in power to bring healing to others. Jesus was anointed to heal! This is how Jesus wrought miracles as a Man. Yes, we know that Jesus in person was and is the Son of God, but in ministry power on this earth, He was a Man. Otherwise, it is entirely useless for us to attempt to duplicate His healings here on earth, if He acted as deity. It's stupid to write books of this nature, then. But thankfully, Jesus did what He did in the name of healing as a Son of Man, thereby showing us that we, too, can be anointed to heal, after being filled with the Spirit and being tested.

> *"...How God anointed Jesus of Nazareth with the Holy Spirit and with power, who went about doing good and healing all who were oppressed by the devil, for God was with Him."* (Acts 10:38)

But we are admonished by the same Man to "...beware of the leaven of the Pharisees and the Sadducees" (Matthew 16:6). What is that leaven? Well, today it is the spirit of antichrist (that just means, "anti-anointing," and specifically anti-healing anointing) that maintains Jesus Christ has changed, even though Hebrews 13:8 says, "Jesus Christ is the same yesterday, today, and forever." The leaven of the Pharisees and Sadducees attempts to limit the expression of Christ (anointed to heal) by changing His image and person to the people, by making Him something other than what He is: a Man intent on giving out the healing anointing to hurting mankind.

I will maintain till my last breath that people who profess Jesus is no longer actively desirous to heal physically today are people possessed of an antichrist spirit. It is the single greatest deception the world has swallowed, and it takes a discerning of spirits to root out that spirit of antichrist, which is one of the primary purposes of moving in panoramic operation.

> *"The former account I made, O Theophilus, of all that Jesus began both to do and teach, until the day in which He was taken up, after He through the Holy Spirit had given commandments to the apostles whom He had chosen..."*
> (Acts 1:1-2)

What Jesus began both to do and teach didn't stop. It had just begun, and was continuing... Luke's Gospel recorded what He started; Acts recorded how He continued through His people. And Acts just ends, right in the middle of the story. There's no final verse stating, "And, lo, it was done, ya'll: finished, *caput*: so don't expect these kinds of acts anymore, folks. Move along now." Something like that would've been important enough for the Lord to insert that one little sentence at the end, don't you think? "Behold, this is how things *were* done, but you guys get left out of it. Sorry."

No, common sense dictates (I'll let that loaded statement hang in the air...) that the works of Jesus continue to this day; if salvation continues, so does healing. For what were the works of Jesus? What was recorded time and time and time again throughout the Gospels? That's right... physical healings, deliverances, blind eyes opening, deaf ears hearing, crooked bodies made whole, flesh-eating diseases reversed.

If all that has ceased, how are we assured salvation of the soul is for today? What if that ceased too, and you and I have no hope? But see, this is what happens when we pick and choose which parts of the Bible are still relevant for today's world. To me, one of the greatest signs that salvation has come for the spirit is that the same God bringing salvation has also brought restoration for the body. Think about that. Healing points to the fact that you and I can be saved spiritually! Otherwise, what's the point of Jesus healing all those people in the Bible? To show them they could also be saved from hellfire, the visible proof of the invisible new birth. That is why healing is such a wonderful evangelistic tool! It's a sign that points to salvation for eternal life.

The purpose of the healing anointing is to convey the works of Jesus, to set people free in their physical bodies, to destroy yokes in their very flesh. People are bowed down by burdens of disease and infirmity, great loads placed on their shoulders called cancer, diabetes, cripplings, maimings and pain.

> *"It shall come to pass in that day that his burden will be taken away from your shoulder, and his yoke from your neck, and the yoke will be destroyed because of the anointing oil."* (Isaiah 10:27)

It is only by activating this healing anointing that these kinds of yokes are destroyed. One way of activation is through panorama— there are others, of course; but for the purpose of this book, of wedding the healing anointing to a prophetic unction: we are studying just how a seer operation can jumpstart that healing anointing Christ has poured into His people.

There are concepts, or laws, that govern the activation of the healing anointing. First, the anointing is activated because of God's calling, as in the case of Acts 10:38, we see "power" was housed in the body of Jesus. Mark 5:25-30, Matthew 14:34-36 and Luke 6:17-19 provide examples of the power resident inside Christ going out to heal the sick.

This power, the healing anointing, is a heavenly material, a spiritual substance. It is transmittable, measureable and tangible, kind of like electricity in our plane of existence; and in fact, "power" is *dunamis*, where we get the word "dynamite." *Dunamis* is inherent ability, power to reproduce itself, but it demands constant use or it wanes away.

"Now Elijah took his mantle, rolled it up, and struck the water; and it was divided this way and that, so that the two of them crossed over on dry ground" (2 Kings 2:8). Notice the cloak absorbed the anointing.

Secondly, the healing anointing is received and activated through one's faith, which is an expectation based on revelation. Healing is based on two conditions: the degree of healing power administered (releasing) and the degree of faith that gives action to the power (receiving). This is why making a demand on the anointing is so important. The healing anointing may be released, but it can be made inert, passive, if it is not received with activating faith. It is more than just a curious touch, an incidental touch, of the Lord's hem—it is a faith touch that energizes the anointing. Faith gives action.

"And He said to her, 'Daughter, your faith has made you well. Go in peace, and be healed of your affliction.'" (Mark 5:34)

Apart from sovereign grace healings (usually as a tool to bring in the lost), just because the healing power of God is present, it doesn't guarantee you'll be healed. In the above account of the woman with the issue of blood, for Jesus to have noticed that power left Him in the midst of the throng tells us that there was resident power to heal everyone present. Yet only the woman was healed because of her faith. Only she made demand on the healing anointing and pulled on the Lord's garment.

Notice in Luke 5:17-26, the account of the paralytic being healed by Jesus, it says in Verse 17, "the power of the Lord was present to heal them." This was *before* the paralyzed man came on the scene—God must have wanted all of them present to be healed, but sadly only one man was raised up when Jesus "saw their faith" (Verse 20).

In Mark 6:1-6, it doesn't say that Jesus marveled at the lack of power, but rather, it was their unbelief that caused them not to benefit from the power that was present to heal.

One's need for healing does not cause the healing anointing to manifest itself for the need. One must make a demand on the anointing—this is true for an individual or for a crowd. Unbelief will stop the flow of the anointing. The purpose of panorama in releasing the healing anointing is to discern the cause of the infirmity, to raise the level of faith for the person in need, and to provide an encounter where the person can then make a demand on the anointing for their healing.

Jesus wasn't able to get people healed unless they believed He was anointed by the Holy Spirit to do so. The hearing of faith comes before the healing of faith. For clarification, read Matthew 14:35

in the King James: notice it was when the men of that place "had knowledge of Him," they brought Him all who were diseased. Now I know the New King James version says, "recognized Him," but the premise is the same: they believed He could heal first, so then they brought Him the sick.

In Matthew 9:27-30, the Lord asked the two blind men, "Do you believe I am able to do this?" When they responded in the affirmative, He told them, "According to your faith let it be to you."

This teaches us a principle of faith that can be incorporated in panoramic operation from the understanding of raising the people's level of belief: see, faith can receive from God whether or not the healing anointing is present. Isn't that a powerful concept! It may take a little more faith application, yes, that's true. But we can lay hands on anyone in faith and see results.

So experiencing panorama increases the corporate level of faith to see healing, even if the healing anointing is not flowing out to them as a specific individual. This is why people get healed in their seats at healing meetings, and no one's laid hands on them.

Now, it's a little easier for the person needing healing when they are standing with someone anointed with virtue, but that doesn't negate the mandate for the person to receive the anointing and mix it with faith.

It's important to understand the spiritual premise of the anointing in its many facets to benefit the most from a panorama release. It is the mixing of all these factors that brings down the applause of heaven.

I said before the anointing is a spiritual substance; it is not a soulish product. That is to say, our minds, wills and emotions can be hindrances to the flow of the anointing. The release of the anointing is from the spirit, down in the belly, flowing out from compassion and love toward the person being ministered to. We should desire to feel love rather than power, and remember that one cannot force the anointing, one can only let it flow. But in all this, we must remember that the anointing must saturate, cover over, completely envelop the person we are ministering to.

The concept I want to convey concerning the ministerial anointing is the necessity of condensing it, of "thickening" the oil, so to speak, so that when it is expressed, it covers over the person we are ministering to. It cocoons them, enshrouds them in a shell of concentrated authority and power. This is the beginning, foundational experience for panorama. The ministerial anointing must be intensified, distilled, and compressed upon a particular need. Experiencing panorama is one type of this amplification, but the primary way of concentrating the anointing comes in being still before the Lord, waiting upon Him, sitting in His presence and cultivating that sensitivity to His Spirit in the quietness of the secret place.

One of the reasons we do not see the release of God's power when we should, at the level that is required to meet the need, is because the anointing is "thinned"—thinned by a lack of understanding and teaching, thinned by operating out of our own reserves, instead of tapping into the limitless anointing of Jesus, but most importantly: thinned by a lack of holiness, humbleness, brokenness.

The question became, how could I have repeat occurrences like the experience in Manchester, regular events of me getting out of the way in the soulish realm so the Lord could move how He wanted to? Where my limited anointing was covered over by His unlimited anointing. What were some keys to see that regularly happening? Trust me when I say I've in no way attained to that level. I'm certainly not there. But the Lord is working, reprogramming, and restructuring. I began asking Him how to translate this revelation to others and their ministries.

My nervous exhaustion breakdown, while not orchestrated or created by the Lord, became a tool He used to begin teaching me one of the most vital keys to this connecting of the anointings: the paramount importance of humility in the anointing. That's not a popular subject: contrition and humbleness before the Lord. It is often conveniently overlooked in many of His servant-leaders today. That's a strong statement, and I stand in the ranks with those of whom I am speaking—but it doesn't negate the truth of God's admonition to us:

> *"But on this one will I look: on him who is poor and of a contrite spirit, and who trembles at My word."* (Isaiah 66:2)

Many of us do not know what it means to be truly humble and continuously broken before the Lord. To tremble when He speaks. (Seems to me we do not tremble as much anymore…) We humble ourselves for salvation, we humble ourselves in times of great need, but as a day-to-day walk of life… well, not so much. But true joy comes from that stance of being crushed before Him in meekness and repentance. We know the concepts, but sometimes we err in the execution of those concepts. It took adrenal fatigue syndrome to remind me just how completely reliant and dependant I was on His grace to function in ministry. So it was one of the crucial keys He revealed to me after the experience in Manchester. It is important to understand, if we are to garner the applause of heaven, so let's take a bit and study humility in the anointing.

THE JOY OF HUMILITY

H UMBLE YOURSELVES IN THE SIGHT of the Lord, and He
will lift you up" (James 4:10).

It's an odd concept: joy in the midst of humility. But it's quite true. Remember when David sinned and wrote Psalm 51:12? "Restore to me the joy of Your salvation..."

In olden days, a truly penitent person wore sackcloth and poured ashes on their head. They rolled in the dust to show their humiliation at their transgressions against Almighty God. Often they would rend their clothes and tear at their beards with their hands. Now, folks, that's some serious repentance. I don't know about you, but I'm not sure I've ever been *that* sorry for my actions against the Lord. And, look, I'm not saying we need to pluck out our beards and walk around in burlap bags with last night's fire remains on our heads; but these were all outward signs of deep mourning, coupled with abstinence from food and the shedding of heartfelt tears of unfathomable regret. Just how sorry are we for our sins? Just how humble are we in the sight of the Lord? That means in His eyesight, before Him, where He can see it (and at times in the sight of fellow mankind as well!).

Bottom line is, no matter how our sins affect other people (and they most certainly do) we are called to account by Him, for it is against Him, and only Him, have we sinned (Psalm 51:4). The story of the prodigal son shows we have sinned against heaven: "I will arise and go to my father, and will say to him, 'Father, I have sinned against heaven and before you...'" (Luke 15:18).

Have you ever actually stopped to think about that? You, yes, you, have sinned against the Creator of the world. THE Supreme Being. You disrespected His laws, and it angered Him. You prodigally squandered the wonderful resources He gave you in eternal life, security, peace, wealth, joy, happiness and health. You were sentenced to never-ending death and torment, the same as demons and fallen angels. That, in and of itself, is thoroughly humbling.

And then, add to that the better news that He *wants* to forgive you, He wants to pardon your mess and bring you to Him, to fall on your neck and kiss you. He commands the best robe to be placed over your shoulders, a ring to be placed on your hand and sandals on your feet. They eat the best beef and make merry, because you were dead, and now you're alive again.

He wants this so badly. So much so, He permitted His only begotten Son, who is also very God Himself, to be executed just so that His blood could pay the price for the sins you committed against Him in the first place. Now *that's* humbling.

So when the penitent received his pardon, he stood to his feet, shook off the dust, and changed into his nicest clothes. Why? Because the Lord Himself swore by Himself (nothing higher to swear by, see?) that He would forgive the penitent and raise him out of the dirt.

"And whoever exalts himself will be humbled, and he who humbles himself will be exalted." (Matthew 23:12)

The favor of the Lord is given to those who are humbled and contrite before Him. Since He is the only one who can pardon our sins against Him, it behooves us to be penitent and self-effacing before Him, right?

If we are, He promises to lift us up, to forgive us as His children, to mend our broken hearts and fill them with gladness, clothed in robes of salvation and righteousness.

Of course, we as born-again, blood-bought children of God understand this, but do we really *get* it? Or let me rephrase that and say, can we ever get it enough?

There is an alarming new movement in charismatic Christendom today. Well, it's not "new." It's actually pretty old, 'cause it finds its roots in antinomianism. What is antinomianism you ask? A term created by Martin Luther (who was very much against the heretical doctrine and wrote a treatise against it—you can read it online), it means "against law." The concept of "lawlessness" was actually addressed by the teachings of Jesus and Pauline doctrine versus Judaism, of course, but it was formalized in the 1500s and given a new facelift.

Luther taught the just shall live by faith, not works; but it got taken too far, much to his surprise, and people corrupted a relatively simple concept (faith not works, the essence of the Protestant Reformation) in having no need to follow moral law at all, because they were saved by faith only—so in essence, it didn't matter what they did, because they "believed" the Lord would save them by faith.

Some went so far as to proclaim their own personal revelation on what they believe they heard directly from God's audible voice was superior (or a "fuller revelation") to the written Word, even though it usurped the authority of, and in some cases contradicted, canonized scripture, which told them to obey the precepts set within it.

Frighteningly enough, we have people teaching a similar concept today, although for the moment, they maintain their further revelation is still subject to the canonized scripture—but that they can add to and increase the concepts presented in the Word of God, and that their revelation is *equal* to Bible. I trust you can see how dangerous this is. One little push, one little nudge from the enemy Deception, and suddenly your "fuller revelation" is higher than the printed Word! I recall a certain group of followers who held a similar belief in their prophet's revelations as they sought to build a temple in Missouri some 180 years ago…

The problem with these kinds of notions of antinomianism and "higher revelation" is they lead to anarchy in extreme forms. And, let's be honest, humanity is usually extreme.

Now, to be fair, most Antinomians maintain that belief in the uselessness of law does not equate to being able to do whatever you want; but the heresy stems from a fallacious notion that God does not demand we behave in holiness, after a particular, clearly defined fashion of righteous living, that includes keeping the laws of the land, unless they contradict our freedom to share the gospel (see Acts 4:19-20 and Acts 5:29), for you cannot love your neighbor as yourself and disregard the laws of your community. See Romans 13:1-7 and 1 Peter 2:13-17, if you don't believe me. The point is, antinomianism emphasizes the goodness of God only—not the righteous demands of a holy Lord.

Flash forward five hundred years, the name of the game has changed slightly, but the misconception remains. The premise is: we repented when we got saved, right? So why do we need to continue repenting? We were saved already, so it's foolish to keep repenting. In fact, this notion has been taken so far as to say we need to repent of repenting, and that there are evil spirits of repentance! In fact, there are services being held to release people from the "condemnation of repentance." In reality, all this does is potentially open them up to demonic oppression.

Now, look, dear readers, I get where this is coming from. Yes, our sins are forgiven and forgotten; they are removed, according to Psalm 103:12, as far as the east is from the west (in other words, "infinity"). I'm not saying we should be under condemnation for past sins that are blotted out from the remembrance of God. You can go too far the other way, also, and be a miserable, frustrated soul just lying in the dirt. Don't forget the "He will raise you up" part of James 4:10. In fact, to be condemned is to be prideful: it is the pride of hating pride, see? It is false penitence. That's not right either.

However, no matter how renewed we become as new creations, and even though the nature of our sins is obliterated and replaced by the life of the Spirit, four bazillion years from now, when we are with the Lord, ruling and reigning with Christ in the new heavens and the new earth, let us never forget we will still simply be redeemed souls, because God first loved us and took the initial steps of restoring lost mankind to His communion.

There are sins of commission, acts we knowingly and intentionally take that are contrary to Christ's law; but there are also sins of omission, or sins we are guilty of that are unconscious. Just seven verses later from James 4:10, where we are told we will be lifted up as we humble ourselves, we are reminded in Verse 17, "Therefore, to him who knows to do good and does not do it, to him it is sin."

I don't know about you, but I know I am not perfectly in the love of God toward my fellow man at all times, every moment of the day. I can't be, because I'm part of that flawed fellow man—yes, I am redeemed, my salvation is assured, and it is no longer in my nature to sin habitually and arrantly—but it will take me meeting the Lord in the air, my corruptible ("corrupt" being the operative word) body becoming incorruptible, before I am without sin—this is the "mystery" of 1 Corinthians 15, and it isn't all that mysterious. In fact, Paul's pretty clear, my dear friends, exactly what happens to us.

And even then, with my new incorruptible, sinless body, I will be without sin only because Jesus *chooses* to overlook my sins of the flesh body I used to have through His own blood—I will always be a soul that He purchased at a very dear cost to Himself by uniting His God-ness with humanity in the first-fruits of a resurrected, glorified body *for all of eternity*.

Have you ever thought about that? That Jesus chose to be the Son of Man for the rest of time without end so that He could be the bridge between you and the Father. And if He had chosen otherwise, the bridge would have collapsed.

I don't know about you, but I do not always love the Lord my God with all my heart, soul, mind and strength. Yes, I've got the basics down: I'm faithful to my wife, I don't steal or murder, but can I say in every instance, 100 percent of the time, Jesus is first above anything else, even food or drink or life itself? That's tough to say—maybe you have attained, God bless you, but I think the rest of us still have a ways to go! I know I do, 'cause I live with myself...

You know, it is possible to go days, weeks, months and not really have anything to repent of; but it doesn't hurt to ask the Spirit, who convicts the world of sin (see John 16:8), if there is something you need to confess before your Father, to humble yourself in His sight, so you can be lifted up!

Repentance should be a way of life, not a onetime occurrence! It is as much an attitude as an act. It isn't just the forgiveness of the sin—it is the humility it takes, the self-effacement required, to prostrate yourself before the Lord and remember it is only by His grace you are able to do so. That is the greatest cause of concern for this new move of "repenting of repenting." It is the crushing that brings the renewal, and I've noticed quite a few of us (myself included) who could stand a little crushing in some areas of our lives.

It is the reward of repentance we should be seeking in the act of repentance, the promise given, the answer to our problem: the lifting up! Why? Because afterward there is the release of JOY!

Now I'm not going to debate "once saved, always saved"—it's not in the context of this book, and really, we'd just go in circles until Christ returned and set us straight. But I want to point out, that what *if* you can reach a place of being so lukewarm toward the Lord, that He does spew you out of His mouth when you meet Him face to face? (see Revelation 3:16.) Are you willing to take that gamble? None of us know the exact day we will die. Let us not get so complacent and comfortable in our relationship with a holy and just God that we meet that day with unconfessed sin. Don't let unholiness take root in your life. Don't give it any place, any room, even for a minute. Don't make God wait for your supplication! Get on your knees and confess them before your Father in heaven, who *will* forgive you. If you sin, don't destroy yourself over it—repent and allow yourself to be picked up. Don't live a life shackled in condemnation for your past, and also don't live a life shackled in self-righteousness for your future. The kingdom of heaven is at hand, *now*, presently—don't miss it!

Study Matthew 6, the Lord's Prayer, which I've no doubt we can all quote by heart. We'll talk quite a bit about this "secret place" (Verse 6) in the course of the book.

"If then you were raised with Christ, seek those things which are above, where Christ is, sitting at the right hand of God. Set your mind on things above, not on things on the earth. For you died, and your life is hidden with Christ in God. When Christ who is our life appears, then you also will appear with Him in glory." (Colossians 3:1-4)

Note the passage above does not say your life is lost or done away with or discarded—just hidden. What is seen and emerges from that secret place is Christ's life shown through you.

The only way to receive these revelations in activation (that is, the release of the anointing in the magnitude that receives the applause of heaven) is found in the secret place. You can read this book fifty times, but if the concepts are not applied in the prayer closet, the words here will only have minimal impact. Be hidden with Christ in God!

But back to the Lord's Prayer, and the kingdom of heaven, notice Jesus says, "Your kingdom come on earth...as it is in heaven" (Matt 6:10). The very prayer of the Lord Jesus Christ is the kingdom of heaven coming on earth; the righteousness, joy and peace of the heavenly kingdom is to be expressed here on earth. We take that to mean the authority and power of the heavenly realm being manifested on earth, and that is not a wrong notion to have. We are part of a spiritual kingdom that will eventually become a physical kingdom upon Christ's second coming. (Again, the ultra-dominion philosophy is not within the scope of this book, so we'll leave that discussion for another time.)

What I want to point out is, there is the manifestation of the kingdom of heaven when it invades earth, the "coming down" of the anointing to mix with ours. But let us also realize *we* are the earth; our flesh bodies—*this* earth—is supposed to represent the kingdom of heaven. The kingdom *has* come, and it lives inside each born-again person. It is to be released laterally, not just vertically.

So with that being said, what did John the Baptist call for when he announced the kingdom of heaven had arrived? "Repent!" It was the first step to inherit the kingdom.

And just what is the kingdom of heaven, the dominion of God? There is a lot of powerful teaching on the concept of the kingdom of heaven coming down to earth, and I agree with the vast majority of it. However, let us never forget that the kingdom of heaven is *already* here—it resides inside us, and we take it wherever we go. It's not so much bringing the kingdom down as it is releasing the kingdom inside.

We as glory people are the ones ever pursuing for heaven to invade earth, to experience open heavens just as Jesus did. So what is this kingdom comprised of? Well, three key elements of this kingdom are righteousness, peace and joy, right?

> *"Yet if your brother is grieved because of your food, you are no longer walking in love. Do not destroy with your food the one for whom Christ died. Therefore do not let your good be spoken of as evil; for the kingdom of God is not eating and drinking, but righteousness and peace and joy in the Holy Spirit. For he who serves Christ in these things is acceptable to God and approved by men."* (Romans 14:15-18)

Now the context of Paul's discussion here is the laws of liberty and love, and how one's food choices are entirely discretionary by the person's own decisions. But there is also a key definition of this kingdom that stems from the said laws of liberty and love: righteousness, peace and joy.

May I humbly submit to you that the righteousness, and thus following, peace and joy, of the kingdom are all rooted in an attitude of extreme humility and contrition (and repentance)? What is righteousness? To be right before the Lord. To be found without fault before Him, and therefore, in His distinct favor. How can we be right before the Lord? Certainly nothing in and of ourselves, for all our righteousness (self-righteousness, piety and vanity) is as filthy rags.

Incidentally that phrase "filthy rags" comes from an extremely powerful piece of Scripture (Isaiah 64) wherein the prophet is asking for the Lord to come down, to open the heavens and shake the mountains. But why is He angry and hiding His face? Because of sin, unrighteousness and iniquity. But Isaiah says, "We need to be saved." Spare us, O Lord, don't remember our filthiness forever—we need to call on Your name.

Again, if this was a singular, one-time occurrence of saying, "Hey, we're sorry, Lord, our bad!" would the prophet go to such great lengths to outline just how unrighteous we are and how angry the Lord is at such behavior? No, I maintain that Isaiah expected a life-change, a continuation of one's humbleness before the Lord. I also believe that if we were to meditate on this before the Spirit, He would show us that our lives are to be an act of repentance—not toward salvation, for that is by faith and not works, but as fruit meet for repentance. (See Matthew 3:8 and Acts 26:20 KJV.) Our righteous actions, including humility before the Lord, show just how sorry we are for our unrighteous actions. It's not a matter of "are we saved?" but how much "are we changed?"

I believe repentance and the following lifestyle of humility are the initial, primary gateways into the kingdom. So how can we expect to express the kingdom by side-stepping, or minimizing, those gateways? For most of us, the longer we have been saved, the less we recognize that we are still in need of salvation—maybe not for our spirits, but for our minds, wills, emotions and bodies. Remember salvation is a continuing process: you were saved from the penalty of sin (justification), you are being saved from the power of sin (sanctification), you will be saved from the presence of sin (glorification).

If we become complacent (the prime expression of self-righteousness; look it up in a thesaurus if you don't believe me) it is sin, because we know to do good (the fruit works of repentance) and do it not.

I'm sorry, folks, you and I still sin, consciously or unconsciously. We may not lead lifestyles of sin, we are no longer slaves to sin, nor do we give place to sin, but to say we are ever 100 percent without sin denies the continued need of reliance upon He who was never with sin: that is Jesus Christ. We would get to a point where we no longer needed Him or His Spirit in order to be completely "right" before the Lord. See how errant that is? But yet, that is the extreme end-result of downplaying a life of brokenness.

We need continuing repentance and humility before our Lord. We may not be unregenerate, we may not be in danger of hellfire (again, I won't debate that here), but we are certainly hampered in the joy and peace which is to follow the righteousness of the kingdom of heaven! We can all agree to that, because for whatever reason, we are *not* on a large-scale seeing the kingdom of heaven in action. (I mean, as a collective body of Christ—I understand there are hundreds of thousands, perhaps millions, of *individual* Christians who *do* experience the open heavens of the kingdom on a day-to-day basis. But how is that expressed to the world at large— that is, the anointing in operation that draws the lost.)

To be able to cry over one's sins is a sign that one is alive in Christ. It seems a paradox, to have joy and life in the midst of realizing the death of sin, but nothing is farther from the truth. The ability to weep over our sins is a sign the Holy Spirit is within us. Repentance leads to godly grief.

Read about the faithful remnant of Zephaniah 3. Those who are prideful are removed, and joy is put in their place, the joy of a meek and humble people; the Lord Himself rejoices over us with gladness, and peace follows after righteousness; fear is removed. I don't know about you, but I want to be a part of *that* group! Because what happens to the *other* group? They're devoured in the fire of the Lord's jealousy. Not pleasant!

The bottom line is humility is blissful, the joy of new life comes out of contrition and brokenness, it kick-starts the anointing that is the tangible evidence of the kingdom of heaven. The love of Christ is brought forth when we humble ourselves. It is great joy to be humbled before almighty God, for He lifts us up! Repentance prepares the way for the kingdom of heaven.

Without it, we potentially could miss our time of visitation, for we knew not the "things that make for our peace" (see Luke 19:42-44). What things that make for our peace? In the previous passage we see that the disciples shouted their praise "for all the mighty works that they had seen" (Luke 19:37) and rejoiced in the peace that comes with Jesus. What mighty works did Jesus perform? Signs, wonders, miracles, healings, deliverances—all the hallmarks of an open heavens. But who missed them? The religious, arrogant Pharisees who demanded that Jesus silence the disciples. To which Jesus was like, "Are you kidding me? Are you so deaf and blind and dumb? If I were to shut them up, even the stones 'get it'—the kingdom of heaven is at hand—*they* would cry out!" (see Luke 19:40). Yes, it's a paraphrase, but don't you agree it's as if Jesus was saying, "The rocks are smarter than you..." It wasn't mocking; it was disturbing to the Lord, for in the very next verse, He is weeping. It also angered Him, because next He cleans out the temple of those presumptuous, prideful moneychangers who thought it was all right to turn the house of prayer into a den of thieves.

Apathy toward sin inhibits humility toward sin. Most of the time, we don't even know we've sinned—it takes the Holy Spirit convicting us, saying, "Hey, that wasn't right, you know..." We cannot in ourselves create a penitent heart—again, it takes the Spirit working with us as we yield (humble) ourselves. So the excuse of "I can't stop sinning because I can't in myself become repentant," doesn't fly—because what it takes is submission to the Spirit, and that's humbling. See why pride is the root of all sin?

The only way to be repentant is by accepting through faith the gift of repentance from the Lord in the first place, which He purchased for us on the cross. Once the gift is received by faith, it is placed into action by the Holy Spirit's conviction (and if need be, chastisement). Even chastisement is a gift from God, you just don't know it yet (see Hebrews 12:6). God doesn't want to punish us or permit suffering (beyond the reproach of Christ, I mean), but we will be led, either by His eye or the bit and bridle (see Psalm 32:8-9). You now have a choice. Make it a good one!

When we try to justify ourselves (even after our initial salvation experience) we deceive ourselves. It is pride, nothing more. We blame God (self-pity), we take it out on others (abusive relationships), and we're the ones at fault. Only you are responsible for your sins, no one else. Yet if we become sanctimonious, that is "lazy" toward sin, what are we left with but to try and pass the buck, on God or on someone else? "It was this *woman* you gave me..." (see Genesis 3:12). The old phrase your mother told you a hundred times should come to mind: "If everyone else jumped off a cliff..."

The righteousness of the kingdom breeds joy and peace. The kingdom is the expression of Christ's rule on earth, through us, not in a sense of control, but in a sense of release. The anointing breaks the yokes of bondage, setting people at liberty and free-dom. (That's for those out there who think this whole apostolic movement is about power-mongering and putting people under control.) Hey, there's another good passage of what happens to one with "haughty looks" and an "arrogant heart"—take a moment to re-read Isaiah 10.

Back to the point, the anointing is the release of the kingdom, the kingdom comes from righteousness (yielding the fruit of peace and love) and righteousness comes from humility.

Humility was a main characteristic of Jesus' earthly ministry as a Man. He was "meek and lowly" (Matthew 11:29 KJV) but as I've said before, "meek" doesn't mean *wimpy*. It means "humble, gentle, mild-mannered, easy-going, modest."

That's a problem with a lot of ministers (and people in the church, too). But let me preface this next segment by stating that I fully understand the "take out the plank before pointing out the speck" (see Matthew 7:3-5) notion of what Jesus was teaching in meekness. To say one is always humble is to show that one is arro-gant enough to presume so. None of us has attained perfection; we are all striving for just a modicum of the meekness and humility the Lord Himself displayed in total fullness. I preach to myself, in trembling reverence before the Lord, but it *is* a key we should all be aware of.

In my other books I've called this the "prima donna" mentality, and that's probably a terrible term, but the impression remains the same. I am convinced one of the great mechanisms for a greater release of the anointing is directly tied to the level of humility and graciousness prevalent in the person. We are all simply vessels of clay in which the Lord has deigned to house His heavenly treasure (see 2 Corinthians 4:7). We should never forget that we are simply *servants* who are called to lead. Our job is to wash their feet, not the other way 'round. Let us never forget whoever is the greatest is the least and vice versa. (See Matthew 18:1-5 and Luke 9:46-48.) It is the nature of the kingdom of heaven to be exactly backward and contrary to our human thoughts on "greatest and least."

> *"Now there was also a dispute among them, as to which of them should be considered the greatest. And He said to them, 'The kings of the Gentiles exercise lordship over them, and those who exercise authority over them are called "benefactors." But not so among you; on the contrary, he who is greatest among you, let him be as the younger, and he who governs as he who serves. For who is greater, he who sits at the table, or he who serves? Is it not he who sits at the table? Yet I am among you as the One who serves. But you are those who have continued with Me in My trials. And I bestow upon you a kingdom, just as My Father bestowed one upon Me, that you may eat and drink at My table in My kingdom, and sit on thrones judging the twelve tribes of Israel.'"* (Luke 22:24-30)

Now, these *are* the words of Jesus, and as such, we ought to pay very close attention to them, wouldn't you agree? On whom does the Lord bestow His kingdom? The man of faith and power for the hour? Or the one who serves the other?

One of the most powerful revelations the Lord shared with me, one that I am endeavoring to implement every time I get up there to minister, is the fundamental importance of striving for humility and brokenness as a servant-leader. Again, I've not attained, and I'm not bashing anyone else out there—I'm just speaking in generalities here. We need to search our hearts and repent, if need be, of a lack of repentance, a lack of humility and meekness: especially those in the ministry.

We need to do away with this "hot shot" mentality that we've got the anointing and we've got the answers the people need. It hinders the true, unbridled flow of the anointing, Christ's anointing flowing through us and co-mingling with our own.

There's nothing wrong with having a sense of self-worth and esteem in Christ, I'm not saying act like a pansy or a whipped puppy—we are the sons and daughters of God, after all! But I believe those sons and daughters should act like Christ did on this earth: not as a scrawny push-over, but in extreme humbleness and gentleness in our day-to-day actions. Mellow out, dudes! We should be easy-going, not so demanding, not so "rough and tough." I've met some ministers who thought they were double-O agents or something (sunglasses and trench coats at the airport, as if anyone cared, whispering in their cufflink microphones), all in the name of "boldness" in Christ; but really their mentality came across as finicky and whiny. Problem was, they left the people they ministered to "shaken and not stirred." (Get it? Double-O agents? That was pretty clever...)

There are many fellow ministers who have powerful anointings and great calls of God on their lives, and they see wonderful miracles, but you can't stand to be around them. They're complainers. Or else they're unapproachable and aloof. I've met some that are downright disdainful of the people they're sent to minister to.

The opposite of meekness is one who is difficult to approach, to talk to, to ask questions of. The opposite of meekness is dullness in perceiving what is happening in the spirit, yet the emotions are touchy, hypersensitive, carried on the sleeve. The opposite of meekness is the inability to mingle and co-labor with one's fellow brothers and sisters (the proverbial "one-man show"). The opposite of meekness is the inability to be corrected in love, to be lifted up by another, to be open and transparent before the people to whom the unbroken person is sent to minister. That fruit of the Spirit, the goodness, the meekness, the long-suffering, the cordiality and self-effacing, unassuming disposition isn't there.

I think we should just be appreciative that the Lord is using us at all, and that the people have us come to their churches. No matter what, we're all austerely unprofitable servants. If the Lord decides to use any of us to release His grace and glory, it's only by a sheer act of His will, because, let's face it, we're not easy to put up with most times! The commodity of heaven is love, joy, peace, longsuffering, kindness, goodness, faithfulness, gentleness, self-control—all of this singular fruit is to be more highly prized as much if not more than the gifts of the Spirit, the signs, wonders, miracles—for it is the wealth, the very currency, of the kingdom.

See, we're here, as ministers, to *minister* to people (wild concept, I know). That word "minister" is synonymous with "nurse, care for, look after, take care of, wait on, serve, comfort." That doesn't mean "coddle"—it means to prefer them above ourselves. It takes a broken, contrite heart to reflect that kind of ministry, you cannot convince me otherwise, it is in that kind of humility where the greater expression of the kingdom lies.

To minister as Jesus ministered, to acquire the applause of heaven, demands a crushed (not bruised, there's a difference) life. You can fall on the rock and be broken, or the Rock can fall on you (see Matthew 21:33-46). Which way's it gonna be? Either way, you *will* be crushed. And that's a good thing!

THE CRUSHING OF
THE HOLY SPIRIT

I N THE CHURCH TODAY, I have noticed a trend toward seeking
ways and means to generate these glory experiences by our own
initiative or will, seeking after the spiritual phenomena with
a hasty, sometimes rash, abandon. That's not necessarily wrong
or evil, in the strictest sense—I *do* believe we should be pressing
into the things of God with ardent zeal. Otherwise we fall into
complacency.

But I have a rather different take on how these glory encounters, the manifestations of the supernatural, are cultivated and
inspired. To me, instead of pursuing signs and wonders, we should
be simply pursuing a love-relationship with the Lord. Waiting on
Him, ministering to Him, allowing our soulish life to be crushed
and humbled, and thus, allowing the Spirit to move as He sees
fit, instead of trying to whip up an atmosphere conducive to the
miraculous. Preferably we should be creating an atmosphere of
silence before the Lord, where we modestly wait on Him. It is in the

secret place, in silence before the Lord, (hidden in Christ, remember?) in humble reverence, that the greatest encounters with His presence are initiated—not by our own doing, but by an orchestration of the Spirit as we worship Him without an expectation to "feel" something.

Freda Lindsay was a pillar in the Christian healing movement, stemming from her husband's "Voice of Healing" in the 1950s which became Christ for the Nations. I was honored to be seated at a table with her for lunch one day, and we were talking about all the many well-known healing ministers she had known for over half a century—which was just about all of them. She had put a pertinent question to each of them, "What in your opinion is the greatest key to seeing the Lord heal people?" She said they all replied without exception, every single one of those great men and women of God responded, "Silence." Waiting before the Lord, quieting oneself so He could move through them. The miracles create a clamor, not the other way 'round.

In the Book of Acts, all Peter did was preach, and the Holy Ghost merely fell on the people. There was no jumping through hoops and rigorous exercises that stirred up the move. I believe we make it too hard sometimes. I've seen some thoroughly embarrassing videos on YouTube of people trying to manifest these moves of the Spirit, and it's obviously not a genuine encounter that has supposedly come on the people. In reality it is a catharsis that caters to the flesh.

Now, a cathartic release is not wrong, again, strictly speaking—I've said before there can be a cathartic element to a move of God's presence. But these experiences in the Lord are not only "feel-good" moments of laughter or weeping; or where we can be slain in the Spirit only to bounce up twenty seconds later with a "Shaba!" and a twitch that doesn't actually *change* our perspective on life in Christ Jesus. These moments are supposed to revolutionize our lives completely. Yet, if we get up after being "knocked down" by the power, and we're not healed, we're not delivered, we're not *altered* permanently, then we're not experiencing the complete purpose of the God-encounter.

I believe the signs, wonders and miracles come out of an encounter with Almighty God that creates an atmosphere of celebration and excitement, not the other way 'round. The miracles themselves create the celebratory ambiance, not reversed. Often I see churches drumming up an atmosphere of exhilaration, anticipation and, really, agitated frenzy sometimes, in order to create an environment for the Spirit to move. Once more, not necessarily wrong if it is orchestrated by the Lord, but most times, the Spirit is limited in movement and the people leave disenfranchised or confused. "Boy, praise and worship was so awesome, how come Martha didn't get healed?"

What's the point of gold dust, if the people are not changed? It's not just so we can see a cloud swirling before the pulpit and ooh and ahhh at supernatural spectacles. These events don't occur *only* so you can take a snapshot with your iPhone and prove to your unbelieving acquaintances that God exists. They won't believe the picture anyway.

I'm not being hypercritical or bashing any individual experience in the Lord. I want to be very clear: I am not so much a stickler that I demand a distinct chapter-and-verse for *every* supernatural manifestation (although there should be some sort of precedence in the whole context of scripture, otherwise we could say slobbering and barking at the moon is a "God-thing"). But I've pointed out on several occasions in my writings that discernment of spirits is something generally lacking in the corporate church setting. How is that discernment of God's Spirit sophisticated and refined? Through quietness, peace, humility, waiting upon the Lord in the midst of His crushings. For those who give the applause of heaven,

I believe it is the number one thing they are looking for, and the number one thing lacking: extreme humility.

It's not just humility though; it's *brokenness*. We can be outwardly pious and inwardly arrogant. The true expression of humbleness, the kind the Lord responds to with His presence, comes out of brokenness and crushing. It is not a popular subject in Christianity, because the process is extremely uncomfortable in the soulish life, where pride originates—in fact, it can be downright painful. But it's important we spend just a few pages here outlining what I believe is the most imperative process to releasing the manifest presence of God.

Hang in there—the next few pages might seem "depressing," but I assure you the reward is so worth the discomfort. This is actually a book of joy! Once we understand how the Lord works on us and why, we can move into what it means to experience panorama, and with God's grace, garner the applause of heaven!

We as Christians are supposed to be instruments through which the life and power of Christ flows. God intended for the Holy Spirit to reside in the spirit of man, and thus from that stance, the body and the soul would be ruled by the Spirit/spirit. But there is a battle raging in our minds, wills and emotions (collectively called "the soul"), because "the carnal mind is enmity against God" (Romans 8:7). The only way to become a pure vessel for Christ's anointing to flow through is if we are broken and remolded by the Lord. Note, I did not say we are to destroy our souls; they are to be broken and then put back together in sync with the Holy Spirit.

This is a process, a way of life, not simply a one-time occurrence. Luke 21:19 in the King James says, "In your patience possess ye your souls." It does not happen in a moment. Now, the Lord may ramp up a time of breaking or move gradually, depending on the person He is molding—and we can protract a season of breaking by our stubbornness and pride; but there are no quick fixes where it happens one time, and we never need it again. A good allegory for this is Jacob wrestling with the Christophany (see Genesis 32)—he was "broken" and blessed, and he walked with a limp from that day forward.

Without a lifestyle of brokenness we are never in a complete position of submission to understanding God's Word and relating that to others in an expression of His glory; further we are hindered in discerning what the Lord wants to do, and in discerning the causes and motivations of others. We are clouded and divided. No matter how much we beg or "act" rightly, without the soulish crushing, we are limited and inadequate in experiencing the applause of heaven.

> *"But Jesus answered them, saying, 'The hour has come that the Son of Man should be glorified. Most assuredly, I say to you, unless a grain of wheat falls into the ground and dies, it remains alone; but if it dies, it produces much grain. He who loves his life will lose it, and he who hates his life in this world will keep it for eternal life. If anyone serves Me, let him follow Me; and where I am, there My servant will be also. If anyone serves Me, him My Father will honor.'"*
> (John 12:23-26)

Jesus taught that without "death" there could not be a return to "life." Unless the grain dies, it cannot be sown to produce more grain. The Son of Man was glorified, but it required His death first—and we are to die with Christ, right? What death are we talking about here? Physically? Note that the word "life" in the Greek is *psyche* (Strong's #5590), meaning "soul." It is through soulish death, the crushing of the Spirit, that our spirits come to life and produce much grain, fruit, worthy acts in accordance to Christ's glorification. Remember Paul's statement, "For you died, and your life is hidden with Christ in God" (Colossians 3:3), and when he also stated that he died daily (see 1 Corinthians 15:31).

The only reason God chastens whom He loves (Hebrews 12:6; Revelation 3:19) is so that His Spirit can pour out of the breaches He has made in our souls. We always say we have this treasure in earthen vessels (again, 2 Corinthians 4:7); but if we don't break the vessel, how can the treasure come out?

The Spirit starts crushing as soon as we are saved, even before! It is the principal action when one comes to God, and as we grow in Him and become more submitted to His Word, this process of breaking begins to search out every facet of our lives. Many who are saved, I daresay most, perhaps *all*, at least in some part of their lives, have areas not relinquished to the Lord, so the battle begins. Is it possible to minister and be unbroken? Sure, people do it all the time; it's one of the reasons for writing a book like this. But the expression is a mixture, or the ministry is driven by a creative mind or a sheer force of will, explosive emotions, fluff. Yes, we are created in His image with great creative potentiality—and that's not wrong, to be creative—but in the ministry of Christ through us, we still must surrender.

> *"Now do not be stiff-necked, as your fathers were, but yield yourselves to the Lord; and enter His sanctuary, which He has sanctified forever, and serve the Lord your God, that the fierceness of His wrath may turn away from you."*
> (2 Chronicles 30:8)

See without that surrendering, it is not the pure work of the Spirit. Operating in ministry solely out of the soulish realm hinders the lasting work of the Spirit, and we are left with half-victories.

Eventually, perhaps after many years, we run to the end of our emotions, our willpower, our physical strength—as in the case of adrenal fatigue—and we come to the realization that it is "not by might, nor by power, but by His Spirit" (Zechariah 4:6). We realize we are not supposed to walk by flesh, but by the Spirit (Romans 8:4).

Walking according to the Spirit does not negate our souls. It is an interesting dichotomy that God chose to work the spirit through the soul and out the body, instead of just directly by our spirits. Yet without it, we would not be broken and would remain stiff-necked toward the Lord. So by forcing us to minister with a physical body through our natural senses, it requires our spirits, by His Spirit, to rise up and subject our personalities and bodies so the personality of Christ shines forth.

God uses the trials, tribulations and yes, sufferings, of daily life to break up our soulish hindrances toward His Spirit. I trust in your spiritual maturity that you realize I do not mean God puts sickness or disease upon us so that we might become broken before Him. The very nature of a healing ministry is to remove physical infirmity (and soulish, too). Our battlefield is between our ears, and in our emotions—it is the enemy that seeks to destroy our bodies (and souls, yes). But the Lord will permit circumstances in our lives to bring us to the place where we realize we cannot even function without His guidance and strength. "Where to now, Lord? I won't even presume to know." We have no more self-love, no more pre-conceptions, we just need Him. So we stagger into the secret place and just sit silently before Him. Waiting. Now He can use us more powerfully than ever before!

The bottom line is there is a law of brokenness. We cannot change God's mind on the subject, so stop trying. Even the disbelieving are being relentlessly pursued by the Spirit who is *desperate* to break them before it is too late. How much more so is that same Spirit pursuing *us*, His children?

Of course, there is discernment required. Always discernment. Is this a chastening of the Lord, or is this an attack of the enemy? People with stage four cancer are not being chastened in love by the Father, but it can be (not always, of course) a result of pulling away from the crushings of the Spirit in another facet of life. If one's finances don't permit the purchase of beans to feed one's children—it's not God's will. On the other side of the coin, those with financial pressures, those constantly being in a state of utter reliance upon the Lord to make ends meet, are often mightily used by Him. The stretching of their faith increases their expectations for God to touch others. Extreme, luxurious comfort, wasteful comfort, can be awfully detrimental to the flow of life through our spirits. Not saying we're not supposed to be well-cared for in this life, not saying we shouldn't have a prosperous journey—don't misunderstand—I'm saying, the Lord uses the day-to-day struggles to break us. Indeed, if you feel like you're being pressed, at least in some area of your life, then, hey, chin up—you're doing it right!

So often we equate every bit of discomfort in our lives as "weapons of the enemy," and quite regularly—more than we realize—it is the hand of the Lord chipping away at the soulish life. We spend hours and hours beseeching the Lord to remove these difficulties, these crushings, not realizing it is the key to our success, the release of His blessing, His anointing. Stop doing that!

You'll see just a bit later in this book how discernment is one of the most powerful, and lacking, keys to experiencing the applause of heaven. Our ability, in whatever fashion we hope to serve the Lord in ministry, to discern the Spirit, the spirits, and the person standing in front of us will determine what level of success we see. How we understand and perceive the person in need, the root cause of the issue, the underlying problem that most likely he or she doesn't even know, is directly related to our level of perceiving spiritually through our crushed senses.

What hinders discernment more than anything I've found is an unbroken soul. Everything is clouded, muddled, filtered through a supercilious mind and egotistical emotions.

For reasons He knows, the Lord God has, in a fashion, limited His limitless power by working through man. He has chosen, in His infinite grace and wisdom, to co-labor with His greatest creation in sanctifying and saving His greatest creation. Neat thought. I may not fully understand *why* He's chosen this way, but it is what it is. If He had not decided to limit His expression through man—to man—through Man (Christ Jesus, who displayed the Father limitlessly because He was completely broken), we would have no capability of being crushed by His Spirit, and this is what we dreadfully need, whether we will admit it or not. It is in our best interest—and really, we have no choice—as the church of Christ to allow the Spirit to break us and shape us, so we can be the vehicle God has called us to be in expressing Himself to the world. And if we have failed in any capacity of that expression, it is precisely due to our stubbornness in striving against the crushings of the Spirit.

That's why I believe this is the single most important concept we as the church need to understand: *the discipline of the Spirit*. It's also one of the least talked about concepts, because it is not popular. But, see, the crushing of our soulish life by the Holy Spirit is not only for our benefit; it takes brokenness to be able to minister to the world at large. This is how the Holy Spirit has chosen to operate, by breaking through our mind, will, emotion, so that our spirits can minister through them, alongside with Him, to a hurting world.

No one likes to be disciplined; it's contrary to our selfish natures. It's uncomfortable. But when the Spirit destroys, He also rebuilds, so that He can pour through us out to others. It's interesting to note that it's not so much the Spirit breaking out, as outward circumstances coming against us, being brought to break the outer shell of our lives. Because He is dealing with the "external man"—the mind, the will, the emotions—He uses external means to diminish those faculties that hinder His flow. In other words, the spirit can rise up and out through our soul and body because the Holy Spirit has caused crushings in our daily lives: the difficulties and circumstances we face which forge an internal strength of spirit (not just emotional resolve and mental determination).

Now the good news is these circumstances, difficulties, trials, tribulations, set-backs, sufferings, crushings, breakings, whatever we want to call them are not accidental. They are orchestrated by the Lord for our own good, and ultimately, the good of those we minister to. It is not by chance, nor because of an indifferent God, we face these struggles. Because the Lord knows us better than we know ourselves, He has tailor-made the perfect hardships and ordeals that will bring about our brokenness in His perfect timing. Often we fail to see Him working behind the scenes of our difficulties, so we blame others for our adversities, even God Himself. The process would run much more smoothly if we did not buck against the system constantly!

God will not stop short. He is extremely thorough in His dealings with us, and He is only satisfied with perfection; that is, the completeness of surrender. Nothing will escape His refinement and careful sifting: even the minute things we pay no attention to. It is all subject to the crushings of the Holy Spirit. He will start with the will (that is His ultimate goal: to possess our wills unreservedly), since that is the very root of the problem, then work out into the mind and the emotions. It is a very specific process that God does not waver from. The sooner we realize, and submit, the better our lives start to become.

The understanding of the work of the cross, dying daily with Christ, nailing our soulish lives to the wood, is not an ambivalent concept, some theory that is unattainable. It is a practicality of being aligned with Him. Only through the breaking can the true works of grace be established. It is not only through His Word and through prayer that we become molded and fashioned into the very image of Jesus—a meek, broken, humble Man who yielded to the Father's dealings without grumbling, without regret, without pride. It takes the crushings of the Spirit.

There must be a division between the spirit and the soul. Most often, when we minister to others, it is a mixture between the two, and we do not achieve the purity of spirit that God is expecting His children to operate in. See, it's not so much power that is lacking in our lives—it is purity. A pure, broken spirit will touch the lives of others much more deeply than a powerfully explosive soul. This is why I look for the humility and meekness, the soft-spoken spirit of a minister more than the loud, hyped-up soulish expression behind the pulpit. Ministry is quiet, deep, abiding. That doesn't mean we're supposed to be dry or boring; it's okay to be bold and outspoken at times. We're at liberty to have a little fun, and *rest* in the flow of the anointing.

Ministry is supposed to be fun; we should be enjoying ourselves, not pulling teeth. And after such gentle expression, then comes the exuberance, the thunderous, boisterous expressions of being released in the Spirit. Often, I find we get it backwards—whipping ourselves into a spiritual frenzy to somehow create an atmosphere for God to move, when in reality we should be stepping aside and simply waiting upon Him with expectation and serene attitudes. That is the division of the soul and the spirit—and it is created in our individual lives as we submit to the crushing inspections of the Holy Ghost.

To mix the soul and the spirit in ministry expression is to create a half-truth, a chimerical mixture, a muddled manifestation of God's power. It taints the purity of the *zoe*-flow of the anointing, and the flesh of the man is on display alongside the power of God. This is sad. I am not beating people over the head with a stick, none of us have attained, and nearly every single one of us earnestly desire only the unadulterated Spirit to come forth in our ministries. But it doesn't change the fact that flesh must be crucified, and this originates in the crushings of the Spirit. Can you see how important it is, then, to allow Him to do His breaking work? Remember Exodus 30:32—the anointing cannot be poured on man's flesh, so therefore, the flesh must be stripped away to reveal the spirit underneath.

> *"And it shall be, whenever they enter the gates of the inner court, that they shall put on linen garments; no wool shall come upon them while they minister within the gates of the inner court or within the house. They shall have linen turbans on their heads and linen trousers on their bodies; they shall not clothe themselves with anything that causes sweat."* (Ezekiel 44:17-18)

Sweat represents a work of the flesh, and it stinks to the Lord.

As the living, active Word splits the bones and slices the muscle of the soulish life, the spirit becomes sundered from the hindrances of flesh; the mind is laid bare; and the emotions and wills which drive our intents are revealed (see Hebrews 4:12). It is only then that we can discern what is of the Lord and what is of our souls.

But it's not just the printed word. It takes the living Spirit to reveal the Word. We can read what the Bible teaches on chastening and suffering in Christ, but without the *rhema* breath of the Spirit, we cannot truly understand the progression. It takes revelation to grasp the process; God must enlighten the eyes of our understanding (see Ephesians 1:18) to see what is from Him and what is from us. All things are naked and open before Him, and to Him we must give an account of those thoughts and intents His Spirit reveals (see Hebrews 4:13).

For those who have read my previous book, you will recall that the glory of God, the manifestation of His power and grace, the anointing that breaks the yokes of bondage, is His *reputation* being entrusted and resting upon us. It is His manifested presence, His indwelling, His *concentrated* omnipresence that can physically be felt with the five senses in the form of a heavy weight. The *chabod* (Strong's #3519) of God, the weightiness, the trustworthiness, the heaviness of His greatness—that is the anointing.

Reference *shemen* (Strong's #8081, oil, ointment, fat, fatness; see Exodus 30:25). The *shemen* of God is represented by the anointing oil, the "fatness" of His great worth and importance, placed upon His people. And it is not given lightly. God thinks very highly of Himself, and well He should. So He is not going to toss His reputation around willy-nilly to a group of people whose own impressions to others are tainted. Our estimation of worth in the people's eyes—I mean, our daily lives reflecting what we teach and preach—is directly linked to the Father's reputation.

This is why we must be so careful to "weep between the porch and the altar" (Joel 2:17). In other words, our daily lives must reflect who we are when we stand behind the pulpit; and if we are not broken, humbled and subservient in both facets, the reputation of the Lord is sullied. His glory is hampered or departs altogether, and we are left *ichabod* (without glory).

I think I've made the point. Thanks for taking the time to read this. It is vitally important, and uncomfortable at the same time. It is the key to the applause of heaven, the key to experiencing panorama. One last thing to point out, before we move onto less somber subjects: this process of crushing cannot be faked or mimicked. True humility and meekness are not feigned, for the whole world sees right through you—God will make sure of it.

Let us recognize we do not possess the virtue of brokenness in ourselves (it's prideful to assume we can be humble without the Spirit). Let us war against the soul, allow the Lord to beat it down, crack it open, and mold it according to His pleasure, not ours. Let us submit to the difficult dealings of a crushing Spirit, and we will have the applause of heaven.

CENTRAL AMERICA

L ET ME SHARE WITH YOU a testimony of how the Lord can reward one's humility. Several years ago I went to a particular nation in Central America. While I don't want to seem vague, I'm reticent to give the specific name, only because this testimony starts out with some of the spiritual leaders of that country being opposed to my ministry expression, in fact, being anti-prophetic. Now, this account has a happy ending; there have been tremendous advancements and changes in the spiritual leadership of this nation: a great progression into the things of God. I want to honor them for that here. Still, some of those leaders are active in the ministry today, and I don't want to bring any embarrassment to them, so we'll just say it was a country in Central America. It doesn't change the intent of the testimony one way or the other.

A large segment of the charismatic, Pentecostal leadership of this nation invited me to come and hold a prophetic conference—I found out later it was one of the first, if not *the* first, of its kind. I remember asking my friend who was coordinating the event, Pastor Ronny Thomason (who's on the board of our ministry and was gracious enough to write an endorsement for this book), "Do they actually realize what they're asking for when they say they want a prophetic conference?"

We didn't know for sure. It's one thing as an evangelist to come down and hold crusades—how vitally important that is! But it's another ball of wax to hold an apostolic/prophetic conference; the dynamic changes significantly just by the nature of the flow of operation. That's not to say it's better or more powerful; I'm just saying it's a different expression, and if the leadership is not under-standing or prepared for it... well, let's just say it can cause some problems, you know?

Turns out they were expecting more of a traditional evangelistic crusade. Yay for me! So here's the first night, and there's at least fifty or sixty key spiritual leaders for the country, including the host of the event, one of the national pastors; and I don't know, a thousand or fifteen hundred attendees. We're in this kind of large high school auditorium—it was packed.

If memory serves, I think I shared an aspect of my testimony, and it seemed the people were blessed by it. But then I stepped down, as I normally do, to call out some people to lay hands on them and prophesy. So the first person stands before me, and through the interpreter, I begin to give a prophetic word of destiny and a word of knowledge. Suddenly I sense this wall of resistance flare up. I couldn't believe it; I'd never felt anything like that before. But I fought through it and called up the next person. The words were very specific, but the resistance was growing more and more powerful as I plowed on.

I sensed it wasn't so much the people that were anti-prophetic. They were hungry; they had no problem with me giving the words of knowledge—I don't think they'd ever seen anything like that before. I remember looking to my right and being shocked at discovering this feeling of opposition was coming from the pastors. The vast majority of them stood up and walked out, religiously defiant. I was utterly crushed.

The service ended, and I felt miserable. The host of the conference called us into his office the next morning to tell me they were shutting down the rest of the event. There were supposed to be two more nights, but he told me they were pulling the plug. The conversation below isn't an exact quote, but this is the gist of what was said:

"We are going to close down the conference." The pastor spoke good English, and it was obvious he was quite angry.

"Why?" I asked.

"Because we don't believe in personal prophecy," he told me.

"Wasn't the event advertised as a prophetic conference?"

"Yes, but this is not what we were expecting. We wanted more of an evangelistic event."

"I can do that," I told him hurriedly. "We, too, believe in the utmost importance of winning the lost. We can make a call for salvation—"

"No, we're going to go ahead and close the conference down. We don't support any of this kind of operation."

I sat back for a few moments, stunned. I asked the Spirit, *What do I do here?*

I felt the Lord say, "Go kneel before him, humble yourself and ask his pardon for the miscommunication."

Now, look, my German constitution is not such that allows me just to go kneeling before folks to whom I feel I've offered no offense. But out of sheer obedience to the Lord, I went and knelt before him where he was seated at his desk. It was a test of my will to humble myself like that, let me assure you.

"Pastor, I want to apologize for the miscommunication. I'm here to serve you and your leaders. I wasn't aware of the disagreement here doctrinally. Please forgive me—I take responsibility on my behalf for not making sure this was communicated correctly. If you decide to close down the meetings, I understand, but if you will keep them open, let me assure you I'll serve you in the best capacity I can, sharing what you feel is best for you and your people to hear."

His heart softened, which surprised me somewhat. But he said, "All right. I won't close down the meetings. But tonight I ask that you just share your testimony and the ministry time afterward is evangelistic."

I thanked him and agreed. That night it seemed there was a time and a half more people than the first night. They were turning folks away. But only a handful of the pastors came back.

I shared my testimony and gave an altar call. About a hundred people came forward and gave their lives to the Lord, praise God! It was a good service, a great night, but I could tell in my spirit it wasn't all that the Lord wanted. He had called me down here as a forerunner to establish something in a nation that, up until that time, had had very little, if any, prophetic ministry. I hadn't been aware of the dearth of the prophetic before coming to the nation, but now I sensed that the Lord was grieved.

But I purposed in my heart to obey the pastor's restrictions for the final night of the conference. With a heavy heart, I went to bed.

The next morning we returned to the pastor's office, and I saw that he was white as a sheet. He fell down on his knees and grabbed my feet, saying, "I don't want to die!"

I gave Ronny a sidelong glance. *Um, okay, what gives…*

The pastor began to describe a dream he'd had the night before. Jesus appeared to him, very angry. (Yes, Jesus can get angry, and we would all do well to remember such, because it is foolish to upset omnipotent deity.)

I don't recall word-for-word what the pastor shared, but the basic message from the Lord was something akin to: "You harmed the purposes I wanted to establish with My prophet. You have touched My anointed, so I am cutting off your ministry and shortening your life." The way it was conveyed to me by the pastor was, more or less, "You messed up bad. I'm taking you out."

Now, I know some of you may have an issue with the concept of the Lord taking someone's life, and I won't speak for certain one way or the other; but at the very least, *this* pastor believed the intent of the Lord's message was that He was going to take him home to heaven. That's a shocking thought!

"I don't want to die," he said. "Dr. Maloney, I may not understand it, but I want you to operate however you'd like tonight, in whatever prophetic flow you feel led."

Wow. That's humbling, for him and for me! That night it seemed there was double the attendees from the night before; they were still turning people away. Somehow the pastor had convinced the other leaders to return, and I don't mean to be trite or humorous when I say several of them were physically shaking in their seats. I guess he told them the same story he'd told Ronny and me, and they were afraid of dying, too.

I remember the crowd was so vast, I couldn't make out distinctly the person I felt called to minister to, other than I could tell the person was a she. "I need to minister to her," I said, pointing. It took a few minutes to get the message relayed to the right person, and for her to come up front.

It was about a ten minute prophetic word. I shared how a couple nights before she and her husband had been pouring out their hearts' desire for what they wanted God to do in their nation. The Lord revealed several events in her life that I described, and infirmities in her body, how long she'd suffered under them, and that He was healing her. I spoke destiny that she and her husband would have their prayers answered, that they would be used to establish sons, like sons of the prophets that would go into the nations of the world. She was sobbing and weeping as I described this panorama experience the Lord was giving us.

After she returned to her seat, someone whispered in my ear, "That was the host pastor's wife."

I suppose the Lord had relented on killing her husband... And all of this came about because I was willing to humble myself, no matter how difficult it was, before one of the key apostolic pastors of this nation, entreating him and honoring him for the authority God had placed in his life.

Those other pastors really began shaking when I had finished giving the word—they were confronted with the reality of God's panoramic expression. Very cool to see!

You might be surprised to hear about the school of the prophets the host pastor established and ran for years and years before leaving this country and taking up a pastoral position here in the United States. Every May and December he would graduate about a hundred, hundred and fifty, students from this prophetic school. Many of the men and women went on to leave the country and secure key positions in the Middle East, places like Saudi Arabia, where great revivals have started in the homes of the Middle Easterners from the prophetic words they've brought forth.

The pastor has become one of the foremost proponents of the prophetic and apostolic, and his influence in that particular country has forged a move that is spreading like fire to other Central American countries: the need for prophetic evangelism.

Say you love it! I know I do.

WHAT IS PANORAMA?

P ANORAMA, WHAT I MEAN BY the word, is not so easily defined because it is a blending of many operations, but I suppose that is the uniqueness of the flow. Actually, panorama is probably a perplexing term, but it just sort of stuck, so that's what we call it. The concept of Hosea 12:10 implies panoramic visions, and the Greek word translated "vision" is *horama* (Strong's #3705), implying moving pictures in a dreamlike state, or transcendent ecstasy (we'll get into that in a bit). Add the prefix *pan*, meaning "all," and we get *panorama*, all-vision. Now, most of us equate the term panorama as a vision that moves, like a film, and that's true; it does include that. But when I say panorama I mean more than just moving visions: I mean it as "all-vision," vision in all its capacities, in many angles.

More than anything, panorama is a discerning of spirits operation. As 1 John 4 admonishes us, we are supposed to test the spirits. Panorama helps in this area, as it is an anointing to distinguish and discriminately identify activity in the spiritual realm, the causes behind any particular type of manifestation, be that demonic or a true operation of THE Spirit. It is not just sensitivity to angels of light or darkness, it perceives the working of the human spirit as well, that which is fleshly. It discerns the root cause of a thing. Discernment of spirits is a revelatory gift, like prophecy, word of knowledge and word of wisdom.

By exposing the activity of the demonic, discernment of spirits is vital to deliverance, but ultimately, this operation's highest purpose is to understand how the Spirit of God is moving, so we can align ourselves with Him. It helps us see and know what the Lord is doing.

It's rooted in the seer flow of the prophetic anointing, but it's important to note that there are levels of "seeing" in the spirit, as is the case in panorama as well.

Firstly, it is a spiritual feeling in one's gut. An inward knowing, deep down, ringing true that you are perceiving what the Spirit is showing. It is part of the still, small voice of the Lord (see 1 Kings 19:11-13) that whispers to our spirits. It is perception and understanding—that is the discernment part—of what is transpiring in the spiritual realm as the operation is active. You *know* that this is not just your thoughts or words or inward vision; it comes from the Lord *through* you, not above you or outside you. It can contain an element of "seeing" with a spiritual eye, but your mind does not physically see anything.

"I speak what I have seen with My Father..." (John 8:38). Jesus' spiritual eye perceived things that His mind didn't always visualize. He *discerned* what the Father was doing, but didn't necessarily see the Father in His spirit.

In this type of inner-vision, this visionary realm of knowing, a person perceives something in their spirit, but their mind doesn't see what they are perceiving. It's the knowings, promptings, nudgings on the inside, and as one begins to speak out what they are sensing, revelation is formed on the lips, the Spirit speaking through their spirit. You just know that you know that you know something.

An example of this type of vision is when you feel you should pray for someone; you feel an inward tug, a longing, a sense of love flowing out toward the person. This type of seeing is not "loud" but it can be intense—an internal desire to see things go better for the person you feel called to, a slight pressure to, say, start up a conversation with someone. You might even sense a sympathetic "pain" in your body for the person's need. It is like Mark 1:41, when Jesus was "moved with compassion." He actually yearned in His guts to heal the leper.

I believe all Christians should operate in this type of communication with the Spirit, developing a spiritual "eye" to perceive what He is saying. Your spirit tells you right or wrong, by the pressing of the Holy Ghost residing within you. The only way to cultivate this sensitivity is in the secret place, waiting silently upon Him, as we discussed in the earlier chapter. It is elementary to releasing the glory of God. Without it, we are extremely susceptible to a false spirit or a human spirit in operation. (Again, we will discuss this more at length in a couple of pages.)

> *"Hear now My words: if there is a prophet among you, I, the Lord, make Myself known to him in a vision; I speak to him in a dream."* (Numbers 12:6)

Chozeh (Strong's #2374) is the Hebrew word for "seer," and *ro'eh* (Strong's #7203) is Hebrew for a "vision."

Panorama, the type of operation I am speaking of, is also photographic. This is a little hard to explain. What I mean by photographic is sometimes the seer anointing works with flashes in the mind's eye, something like still photographs, often one after the other, sometimes on top of one another. Perhaps "montage" is a good term to use. You know, like in high school where you had to glue a bunch of pictures on a poster board to tell about yourself? It's like an inner vision of knowing, but coupled with pictures. Once you see these pictures, you can then describe them. As in, "I see you standing on a ladder. And I see that you fell from the ladder, and I see that you fractured a rib."

The photos don't move, but the seer describes what each photo contains, like a piece of a puzzle, until the entire concept is revealed, almost like a mosaic. Snapshots is a good way to describe it. These photographs can flicker in your brain, just like a memory, or even on the back of your eyelids. The point is the operation is happening internally, in the mind. So by describing what we see in the photographs, there is an element of word of knowledge coming into the mix, as the Lord is showing past events. There is also a word of wisdom gift as future events and destiny are revealed.

The third type of seeing is a moving vision, what we would commonly associate the word "panorama" with, although when I use the term I mean all of these things we're discussing in this chapter combined in varying levels. This is an inward vision in motion, like watching a movie in your mind's eye. Really, it might be a series of pictures unrolling before the seer, but it's in such a way as to give the impression of animation.

The thoughts of the seer stand out in front of them in the natural realm and move, usually from left to right. You still see the floor or the walls or the ceilings, but your thoughts are superimposed in front of them.

Lastly, a vision can be external, which means the moving scroll or the photographs or the vision is outside the brain, just like you are watching a film on a screen. It is seen with the physical eyes, not the mind's eye.

Oftentimes, when people say they have visions, I find it's more of the photographic flow inside their minds. That's not wrong or less important, but it is distinct from having an outward vision impress itself on your physical eyesight, versus seeing something in your mind's eye. I mention this only to show the distinction between the two types of flows, not to demean any one type of operation.

While not everyone moves in the second or third realm of seeing (and sadly, in some cases, not even the first), the manifestation is open to every believer as the Spirit wills. Again, pressing into these kinds of operation should actually be rooted in pressing into a deeper relationship and sensitivity to God's Spirit, not seeking to "see" but seeking to know Him "...that I might know Him..." (Philippians 3:10). Of course, don't forget the context of Paul knowing the Lord in the suffering of the loss of all things and having yet not attained! This is a type of crushing.

Okay, back to panorama. As I mean it, it is the merging of all of the above functionalities: you feel, discern, know, see internally. Mostly it covers over you in a cocoon, like the "pillar vision" I mentioned awhile back.

Also mixed with this seer operation in its varying levels is a download of a gift of faith (see 1 Corinthians 12:9). Now, as you are most likely aware, a gift of faith is externally given from the Father—it is an element of the Father's faith mixed into yours. It is not a permanent faith, and it lifts off once the operation is complete. It is not your personal level of faith, the faith you have toward God, which is supposed to grow and mature, starting as a mustard seed and turning into a shade tree.

As I stated before, I don't believe any of us have (and I question if we can) achieved a level of faith in our relationship with the Lord to see creative miracles take place apart from a gift of faith dispatched from the throne. I believe as we see healings happen it encourages our own level of faith to believe that the next person can be healed, but this primarily revolves around internal needs, be those emotional (inner-healing, deliverance) or physical (tumors, diabetes, broken bones and also deliverance from spirits of infirmity).

But when it comes to a creative, or recreative, miracle, I believe it takes an extra unction of God's faith being imparted, otherwise what is the point of a gift of faith? When you or I are faced by a person with an amputated foot, do we have the kind of faith required to see it just miraculously grow in front of everyone's eyes? After almost forty years as a healing minister, I can honestly answer no. I am reliant upon the Lord's faith in Himself to see toes grow, or eardrums created, or eyeballs replaced. That is a higher level of the miraculous that we are all pressing toward, but honestly not seeing on as grand a scale as we should. Again, I want to imply corporately as the body, not individually.

Next, there is a straightforward prophetic element to panorama, speaking forth the word of the Lord in a *nabiy'* (Strong's #5030) flow, the bubbling of a fountain of words, what we would traditionally accept as a prophetic word being given to a person that is communicative in nature. There is the element of dropping words like dew (*nataph*, Strong's #5197). There may be a burden of the Lord pressing down, requiring release (*massa'*, Strong's #4853). These are often associated with giving prophetic declarations, over a corporate body or even a nation, although all three flow and interchange. There can be an audible voice of the Lord also in this operation.

These are the manifestations most commonly connected with prophetic ministry, and each has their place in a panoramic flow, since we mean it as "all-seeing, all-inclusive." Any type of intense movings of the spirit of prophecy (see Revelation 19:10) can be panoramic; it's just a higher order of transcendence, coupled with an ecstatic sensation, which we'll discuss next.

While operating in panorama, there is often a heightened, transcendent experience for the person operating in it, and the person receiving it. Now this will rub the anti-"altered state of conscious" people the wrong way. I always see the nay-sayers blasting the "trance" teaching from charismatic Christians. But it is what it is. There is ample biblical evidence of being "caught up" in a state of rapture and bliss. (See Numbers 25; Mark 5, 16; Luke 5; Acts 3, 10, 11, 22, where the words "trance" or some form of "astonish" or "amaze" is used.)

While I strongly caution everyone not to institute a similar kind of experience for themselves, the Lord does initiate this kind of "lifting up" encounter frequently in a panoramic operation. Most of us know the Greek word is *ekstasis* (Strong's #1611), where indeed we get the English word "ecstasy." Literally it means "to stand beside oneself." One's body is short-circuited by the power of the Spirit, and the person is physically held in a state of stupor. When one is "slain in the Spirit" or "falls under the power"—and I mean *really* falls under the power, where they don't bounce up four seconds later as if nothing happened—this is a type of *ekstasis*.

All of the above entails what I mean when I say "experiencing panorama." But perhaps it's better to point out a couple things I think panorama is *not*, and that might, hopefully, clarify what we're talking about.

I've noticed a teaching in charismatic circles that maintains there is no real distinction between the preternatural and supernatural realm. It seems to me it's becoming more prevalent in teaching among our Christian groups that there is the natural realm; that which is experienced through our five senses, the earthly realm we live in currently. And there is the realm of the spirit, God's realm. It is also taught that these realms are relatively neutral—not inherently evil or inherently good—they just *are*; and it is the beings residing in them, earthly or spiritual, that can be either good or evil (angels versus demons, etc).

Now there is truth in the notion that the earthly realm is not inherently evil. When the Lord created the heavens and the earth, they were good, and still are. However, this earthly plane of existence has become corrupted by the devil's fall and man's original sin. For me personally, the corruption of the earthly realm has more to do with Adam's fall and subsequent relinquishing of the *rule* (stewardship responsibility) of this earth's system to the devil. (Not the earth itself. That belongs to the Lord according to the Bible in Psalm 24:1.)

Hang in with me here for a couple of pages. My point in sharing all this is to highlight the importance of threes in the Bible. We are spirit, soul and body (three). God is trinity (representative three, in essence one: you'll have to wait for *Aletheia Eleutheroo* for the teaching on this). Noah's ark had three levels. There are three parts of the tabernacle: the outer court, the holy place and the holy of holies. Jesus raised three people from the dead in scripture, and He Himself was raised from the dead on day number three. In other words, three means something to God.

Paul talks about being caught away to the third heaven (see 2 Corinthians 12:2-4). It is generally accepted that Paul is speaking humbly of himself as the "man in Christ," but what is the third heaven? It must imply a first and a second heaven, correct?

Well, the second heaven is parallel to the first heaven, an unseen realm that runs alongside the seen realm. The second heaven is on the physical earth unseen, a spiritual plane of existence.

The first heaven is the earthly plane of existence, our world, the cosmos, space, the stars, the planets, the "natural" or "seen" realm. The second heaven is corresponding to the first, that which is called the preternatural realm, and it is "unseen." Preternatural means "outside nature," but it is a distinct notion from supernatural, which is "above nature." The second heaven is where the devil and his demons reside, but they can manifest in the first heaven, as shown by Lucifer being cast to this earth (see Revelation 12:9). The preternatural realm is a spiritual, unseen realm, meaning an earthly physical body cannot live in it, but it is not the realm of THE Spirit. The Hebraic understanding of Abraham's bosom, paradise and hell, *Sheol* and *Hades*, would be a part of the preternatural realm. This is not specifically God's realm, even though it is a spiritual plane.

As far as I know, nearly all Christians agree the third heaven is the realm of God Himself, and in this realm is the New Testament heaven, where a redeemed spirit would go immediately upon death (an unredeemed soul going to hell, *Gehenna*.) This is the throne-room of God, the gates of pearl, the sea of glass mingled with fire, the New Jerusalem waiting to descend after the Second Coming, and so on.

Now why am I talking about all this, when I should be defining panorama? Because I want to show that the seer operation is not supposed to be dealing with the preternatural realm. If we teach there is only the seen realm and the unseen realm, without the distinction of the preternatural and the supernatural unseen realms, we can open ourselves up to a lot of deception. We can easily become ensnared in goofy theology and oppression by tapping into the preternatural realm, assuming it is the supernatural realm of the third heaven.

If we maintain there is only the spirit realm and the earth realm, that the spirit realm is neutral (neither intrinsically good or evil), without a discerning of spirits, we open ourselves up to deceiving spirits of familiarity. I know that's a lot of "spirits" there, make sure you understand what I'm saying.

This is what a psychic does. This is what conjuring the dead in the OT was. This is occultism and witchcraft. This is what New Age philosophy teaches: that it's all one and the same, "God's realm." And it's not! They are tapping into the preternatural realm. And if we're not assured of our source, we as prophets of God can tap into the same mess. We have no business dabbling in the preternatural realm, it will lead to defilement.

Panorama is not this. It does not read your social security number and tell you how much money you have in your bank account. I'm not saying that every instance of such prophecy is rooted in the preternatural realm, but I always question the *why* of God's revelations. Who cares if I had a great-great-aunt named Beth? Or if my middle name is Edward (don't laugh, it was my adopted father's name). Do I get healed or set free after this is revealed? Do I walk out of the wheelchair? Or does the audience ooh and ahhh, and I leave unchanged?

Now is panorama specific like that? Yes, it is. But there is always a reason behind such a revelation. The bottom line is panorama exists to breach the spirit realm, the third heaven, and root out the fallacy of operating in the second heaven.

The last several pages of this book have been dealing with pressing for supernatural encounters at the expense of creating a relationship with the Lord, in rest and silence, waiting before Him. The preternatural is the false shortcut to experiencing the true (pure) realm of the Father. This is why panorama is 99 percent discerning of spirits.

Panorama is a type of plumb line, an established link between the first and third heaven, bypassing the second. For those of you who read my first book, thanks! And recall, please, the pillar dream I was describing, wherein a cloud of glory came down upon me (that's the descending anointing) and the person I was ministering to, cocooning and bubbling us, shielding us from the outside. Nothing "funky" could penetrate, and since the pillar was not hollow, it went through us, so nothing on the inside could contaminate the pure flow of the Lord. It was like being entirely under the control of the Spirit. *This is panorama*, and on many occasions I, and the person being ministered to, have seen this cloud, like the one in my dream, descend when the Lord operates in this manifestation.

Not tootin' my own horn here; remember, this isn't *me* at all—that's the whole point. After the adrenal fatigue, I can barely minister as "me" anymore. So God Himself gets sole credit for this activity. But I do believe there are principles we should all adapt and implement in our ministries, at whatever level we have, to see a similar type of operation, if not exact. I believe the Lord is bringing us into a season where this type of seer operation is going to become more prevalent in our times of ministry.

It has to, as far as I'm concerned. Just like the sons of Issachar had an understanding of the times, to know what Israel ought to do (see 1 Chronicles 12:32), one of the main purposes of panorama's discerning element is to define the times in which we are living, to understand and perceive, to better equip the people (spiritual Israel) to know what they ought to do.

The greatest of God's gifts to His people, in this context, are *opportunities*. We are told in Ephesians 5:16 to redeem the times, because the days are evil. In order to redeem the times we live in, we must cultivate a sensitivity to the occasions that God has created for us to press into ever-deepening expressions of His manifest glory—that is a surefire way to gain the applause of heaven. Panoramic anointing develops this sensitivity to perceiving the times.

As you know, the Bible presents time linearly, not so much cyclically. What I mean by that is time began at creation, and it will end when God's purposes are accomplished on this earth.

Then time will cease to be. There is a definite quantity of time, a fixed beginning and a fixed end. God already knows that end, when time ceases. In the midst of this natural, linear flow, what the Greeks called *chronos* (Strong's #5550), God has inserted moments of special times (*kairos*, Strong's #2540), seasons of His specific purposes intersecting *chronos*. These are the "opportune" times, the "right" moments, the "favorable" seasons in the midst of day-to-day activity.

These *kairos* moments are divinely foreordained periods of God's intervention, or they can be created on the spot: times of God's moving because we have made ourselves available to minister to the needs of the people. These moments interrupt normal time with an explosive expression of God's power and purposes being established. These are what the sons of Issachar could perceive, and therefore, instruct Israel on how to capitalize on those moments. This is why cultivating the discerning of spirits, the release of panorama in this age, is so important: to distinguish and perceive the "now" moments, those special opportunities, of the Lord; for what we do and establish in this lifetime propels and confirms the purposes of God for the lifetimes that come after ours, so that *chronos* is completed.

Panorama helps us enter into those purposes of God, for we can only enter in when we have an understanding of what we're supposed to enter into. Makes sense, right? This kind of seer operation simplifies and distills the purposes of God for a given moment in time. It shares the *kairos* of eternity's plan within earthly time, that decisive unveiling of the eternal element of God's objectives. It is a cultivated sensitivity to "catch the scent" of what God wants to do; it is a quickened understanding.

We have to catch God in the very act of intervention, so to speak. Panorama helps reveal the God who inhabits eternity, the God of Ages who is breaking forth into the time of men with a new expression of His limitless glory. See why it's important to have an understanding of the times? I'd sure hate to miss one of these *kairos* moments. Wouldn't you?

The operation of panorama generates a fully sensitive awareness of those created, appointed times. It helps form a sense of identity in the people. You've got to realize you are no accident: you have been brought to this precise moment in *chronos* in order to lay hold of the special opportunities that this *kairos* is presenting. When God called you to repentance, He called you to ongoing purpose. Your life *started* at salvation, and you have a goal to attain, that which acquires the applause of heaven. You are not just born again to be born again. God has already completed your purpose in His will, and now you must execute it. The manifestation of panorama can help you.

First Peter 5:6 says if we humble ourselves under the mighty hand of God, He will exalt us in due time (*kairos*.) Galatians 6:9 tells us not to become weary in well-doing, for we shall reap in due season (*kairos*) if we don't faint. We shall become possessors of unfulfilled prophecies, the inheritors of the blessing, and in turn, the power to proclaim the blessing to others.

The function of panoramic operation is to instill a sense of self-worth for the recipient. "It matters that I am alive." They are called to a place of honor where they will sacrifice for truth and what they're called to do. They begin to understand that God carefully made them unique so they might serve Him in a different manner than anyone else alive—they have something to give to God and to mankind that no one else can give. They have a purpose; they begin to know why they are put on this earth. Leadership traits surface. Because of an implanted sense of destiny, the receiver is able to withstand trials; the end result of what they are called to do and to be is worth any cost. Faith is increased because now they *know* God desires to use them. Each person has greater depth and insight "downloaded" into their spiritual mainframe, giving historical vision but for future implication. "I'm here at this time in history to serve His purposes for my generation, and what He has put in me, in turn the next generation must have in order that they may do greater things." It is an exponential gifting. And it is a gifting that speaks to nations—let me tell you about Jordan.

JORDAN

I N THE MID-NINETIES, I HAD the distinct privilege of traveling to Amman, Jordan, with one whom I consider a mentor in the faith, Dr. Chuck Flynn. We were going to minister prophetically, which was virtually unheard of at that time in the country.

One particular church we were at hosted about nine hundred to a thousand people. I got up to preach, but the Spirit stopped me and said, "Prophesy."

So I said, "Okay, Lord… which ones are the Christians?"

The Lord gave me a loving rebuke. "Where in My Word did I ever tell you prophetic words were just for My people?"

Right. Duh. So I just stepped out in faith, not knowing who was saved, who was unsaved, and began to follow that prompting to let the bubbling of my spirit come forth. I felt the anointing ascend, and I felt a cloak of God's anointing descend, along with a gift of faith to call out the correct people.

I pointed my finger in a general direction of the audience and said, "There's a woman over there. You have a thirty-two-year-old son." I was describing what I saw in a panoramic snapshot. "He was hit by a truck and paralyzed from the waist down. He is at home in a wheelchair as I speak. Go call him, and you will see he's being healed."

We found out later when she gave testimony that the lady was Muslim. She turned to several of her friends, exclaiming, "How does he know my son is paralyzed?" She went into the church office to use the phone.

Her son told her, "Something is reverberating in my legs. I feel fire in my legs!"

So she raced home and brought her son and husband back. The son was healed, all three were saved, as well as two or three of her other friends, and about five different families she'd brought from her neighborhood, for they all knew the son and that he was wheelchair bound. Praise the Lord!

I called out twelve other people that night, randomly in the audience, and the panoramic words were very specific. After that, I felt the anointing lift, and I didn't feel impressed to minister to anyone else. When the service was over, a lady approached, in tears, and knelt before me, touching my feet. It was a strange thing to do, and I don't know if that's a Middle Eastern custom or what.

But she said, "I am the press secretary for King Hussein. I was sent here by His Majesty with several bodyguards for the express purpose of arresting you, should you have said one negative thing against Islam. I want to tell you that the thirteen people you called tonight, to a person, are employees of the palace and work directly with the king on a daily basis."

Oh, come on, there's no way to do that in the natural! That's what I call a sign and wonder, praise God! Over the next three or four days, those thirteen people (including the lady whose son had walked out of the wheelchair) took their prophetic words and wrote them out in Arabic, taking them before the king to be read.

King Hussein was gracious enough to write Dr. Flynn and me a letter saying, "Please bring a delegation of ministers from America to deliver the word of God as you have done for my employees."

How awesome is that?

"...So His visage was marred more than any man, and His form more than the sons of men; so shall He sprinkle many nations. Kings shall shut their mouths at Him..." (Isaiah 52:14-15)

Everything Jesus went through in His passion was for the purpose of restoring something that was lost by the Fall. Which is why we are healed by His stripes (see Isaiah 53:5) and etc. So the Lord's face being beaten more than any other man's was for the purpose of restoring to us the gifts of the Spirit, specifically the vocal gifts (that is, prophecy, word of wisdom, word of knowledge, tongues and interpretation of tongues; see 1 Corinthians 12). It is prophecy that "sprinkles" the nations. That is why the testimony of Christ "is the spirit of prophecy" (Revelation 19:10).

Now think about it. In order for His visage to be so marred, it would require such physical striking as to render the face just a sack of purple bruises and blood, no form, no distinguishing features, just raw destruction, literally beaten to a pulp. Imagine being struck so many times in the face, bystanders couldn't even tell what you looked like. No, on second thought, don't. The human mind cannot comprehend it.

But all of that was for the restoration of the prophetic—so you and I could operate in panorama for His people and the world. Sobering, isn't it? Do not take prophecy lightly!

> *"Then some began to spit on Him, and to blindfold Him, and to beat Him, and to say to Him, 'Prophesy!' And the officers struck Him with the palms of their hands."* (Mark 14:65)

See, they were mocking Him; they were mocking the word of knowledge. "Who hit You? Prophesy!" Turns your stomach, right?

But when we prophesy in His name, it restores His full cosmetic appearance (I'm speaking metaphorically)—it sprinkles the nations, and even kings are made silent.

The gifts of the Spirit give an avenue for the fruit of the Spirit to come forth. "...A golden bell and a pomegranate, a golden bell and a pomegranate, upon the hem of the robe all around" (Exodus 28:34). It's not either or, it's both: the bell (gifts) and the pomegranate (fruit) that are supposed to hem the garments of His priests.

Why, look at 1 Corinthians 14—prophecy is to bring in the lost! I know Paul says prophesying is for those who believe (Verse 22), but his very next thought is to show how prophecy convicts and convinces, and the unsaved proclaim, "God is truly among you" (1 Corinthians 14:25).

Despise not prophesyings! (1 Thessalonians 5:20 KJV). They were bought with a price, and they may just lead you before kings!

DEVELOPING
PANORAMA

S O WE'VE DEFINED HOW THERE are two unseen realms, the preternatural (which we're not supposed to access) and the supernatural realm (which is *imperative* that we access for the release of Christ's full anointing). This supernatural, unseen realm—the realm of the kingdom of heaven—is all around you at all times. In fact, because the access point to that realm resides in your spirit-man, technically you carry the kingdom of heaven inside you everywhere you go. Truly, the kingdom of heaven is at hand, because a portion of it resides in your middle.

Just because you cannot see something doesn't mean it's not there. We cannot see ultraviolet or infrared light with the natural eye, but rest assured, they're there.

The key is to develop a way of perceiving that unseen realm —creating a realm of "seeing what is unseen." That's the essence of the prophetic and seer operation, and as such, the operation of panorama.

Wanna know why the Jews sought to kill Jesus? Yes, because He claimed to be equally God. But specifically, because He claimed to *see* what the Father was doing in the unseen realm and then mimicked His exact actions on earth, replicating perfectly that which God the Father was working out in the heavens above, a visible representation of invisible activity. So the only reason Jesus healed on the Sabbath, was because He saw the Father healing on the Sabbath, and He simply duplicated what He saw.

> *"But Jesus answered them, 'My Father has been working until now, and I have been working.' Therefore the Jews sought all the more to kill Him, because He not only broke the Sabbath, but also said that God was His Father, making Himself equal with God. Then Jesus answered and said to them, 'Most assuredly, I say to you, the Son can do nothing of Himself, but what He sees the Father do; for whatever He does, the Son also does in like manner. For the Father loves the Son, and shows Him all things that He Himself does; and He will show Him greater works than these, that you may marvel. For as the Father raises the dead and gives life to them, even so the Son gives life to whom He will.'"* (John 5:17-21)

All seers are prophets (not all prophets are seers). And I know we're not all seers standing in the office of a prophet (Ephesians 4:11), but I believe *all* of us, all Christians, should strive to remove the veil that blinds our spiritual eyes and to learn how to cultivate a seer lifestyle out of intimacy with God, just as the Son did. So the question to ask is, where is your spiritual eye?

See, seers (that's funny) experience encounters with God and express what they've seen to the physical world, just like Jesus was doing. They are "now" prophets. What I mean by that is when they see something in the spiritual realm, they speak as though it was happening *right now*, today, not a future occurrence. (Sometimes that's a problem, since what they see is so alive and vivid to them, they can't discern the timing of when it is to happen, if God is showing them something that will occur in the future.)

But there is a principle in the "now authority" of a seer, that ability in a prophetic visionary to decree what they hear and see in heaven as an invisible action and release it into the "now"—the present realm we are in. In other words, they birth a manifestation of God's anointing. These are the signs and wonders of a seer, and this is why I believe the prophetic is so important a companion to the healing anointing. If we do not see the signs and wonders in the magnitude that catches the applause of heaven, it is partially, I believe, because we do not implement the prophetic, and specifically, the seer operation into the miraculous as we should.

We see biblical examples of the prophetic breeding the miraculous in Elijah, and truly Job was a prophet of the open heavens, but perhaps the best example of the prophetic paving the way for the miraculous was John the Baptist, whom Christ called the greatest of the prophets (see Luke 7:28). But again, what was this prophet's word to the people? Repentance.

These types of prophets, and specifically seers, expose the sin motivations of people that hinder the flow of the anointing; they reveal the thoughts and the intents of the heart that inhibit the manifest presence of God. But this is why a prophetic person must be so broken and submitted to the people he or she is ministering to, otherwise, you get the harshness and rudeness of "fault-finding" or abrasive correction that does not stem from a motivation of compassion and love. These are the so-called "judgment prophets." The primary modus operandi of a true prophet is to expand the knowledge of God's love to the people, even in the midst of a rebuke.

Part of the operation of panorama is found in uncapping those prophetic wells, tearing off the hoods that have been placed over people, the blindness of disobedience.

> *"Pause and wonder! Blind yourselves and be blind! They are drunk, but not with wine; they stagger, but not with intoxicating drink. For the Lord has poured out on you the spirit of deep sleep, and has closed your eyes, namely, the prophets; and He has covered your heads, namely, the seers."* (Isaiah 29:9-10)

Rough gig, huh? The prophet goes on to proclaim the whole vision has become like a sealed book, and the people it's brought to are unable to read it, because it's sealed, or because they're illiterate. But Verses 18-19 are a little more exultant: "...the eyes of the blind shall see out of obscurity and out of darkness. The humble also shall increase their joy in the Lord..."

Can the prophetic remove the hoods that blind the people? Can the prophetic break a demonic assignment that keeps people from seeing? Of course it can. But what are a few of the reasons for veilings in the first place? Primarily, it's because of our own stubbornness: we choose only to look at what we want to see.

To be completely honest, most of our churches inhibit the full rein—that's a horse-riding term, not "reign" as in *rule*—of the prophetic. Mostly, we only allow room for edification in the prophetic, if it's allowed at all. We don't *let* the people see! This is why we're admonished to "not despise prophecies" (1 Thessalonians 5:20). It quenches the Spirit...

(And yes, I know there's an additional two commands in the very next verse that says, "Test all things; hold fast what is good," but "testing" does not mean "tossing out"—and we *are* supposed to hold fast to that which is good... Again, discernment. Can't get away from it.)

Let me make a strong statement in love that may ruffle a few feathers here: overly pastoring the prophetic creates a low level of operation.

The context of this whole book shows the supreme need for humility and submission in our gifting. I most certainly believe a prophet is to be submitted to an eldership of peers, of which he or she is a part of; but most people have an incorrect notion of a prophet—that he or she is unable, because they are parabolic and express the "emotions" of God, to be just as balanced or doctrinally sound as any of the other five-fold offices. Prophets are watchers, seers, looking out over the parapets of the city's fortifications. As such, it is necessary, sometimes, for them to be "apart" from the congregation—not saying they should go "rogue"... I'm just saying they should not be unduly shackled.

But frequently, we frustrate seeing in the spirit by placing caps on just what we will see. In Amos 8, we see God sends a famine, not of bread or water, but of the word of the Lord; and everyone runs to and fro seeking it, but it is not found. Let us not be a nation that is famished from a lack of God's ever-proceeding "now" word.

The purpose of seeking revelation, the spirit of wisdom that Paul speaks of in Ephesians 1:17-19, is that we might grow in the knowledge of Him, to know our calling and inheritance, to know the greatness of His power toward us, the believers.

It is that manifold wisdom of God that the apostle is speaking of just a couple chapters later (see Ephesians 3:8-10): the love of Christ, the strength and might and courage and grace, revealed in Him. This is what we miss when we are blinded, my friends. This is what we forgo by capping the prophetic wells.

It is that spirit of counsel and might (see Isaiah 11:1-4) that releases the miraculous; for this purpose are we to "see": so that we might perceive the spirit of counsel and might. It is my firm persuasion, operating in panorama, that the seer anointing breeds miracles. By speaking of what they see, sharing that word from the unseen faith realm, it is converted into a word of healing for the person being ministered to, and thus the miracle is activated. Really, converted is probably a bad word to use; it's all just *the* word. That is, the appropriation of our covenant rights and privileges purchased by the cross—*that* is healing. But the word spoken of what is seen in the unseen realm is a catalyst for the release of that covenant right, watching the Father move and then moving in perfect unison with Him, as Jesus did—it takes an ability to "see" into the unseen.

The thing is, our words are backed up by the signs and wonders. Take note of Hebrews 2:4: "...God also bearing witness both with signs and wonders, with various miracles, and gifts of the Holy Spirit, according to His own will." And read in Mark 16:20: "And they went forth, and preached everywhere, the Lord working with them, and confirming the word with signs following. Amen."

The prophetic flowing forth, especially the vision of the seer being described (as in the case of panorama), helps actualize the past-tense provisions acquired by the broken body of Jesus on the cross; it helps the people being ministered to "stake their claim" on what is already promised them, what is offered by their relationship with Christ. If we are not seeing the provisions manifested as we should, perhaps it is due to a stifling of the prophetic, seer flow? Just a thought to consider.

No ifs, ands, buts or doubts, flat out—the prayer of faith "shall save the sick" (James 5:15). That's why Mark 16:18 is written as a statement of fact: "They shall lay hands on the sick, and they shall recover." No room for any other option, the prayer of faith is 100 percent or nothing. So if it is *not* saving the sick, then it is not a prayer of faith, right? See, because people are not having encounters with God's true glory, those prayers of faith are not breathed upon by Him. They're just letters and incantations, words without power.

Word of Faith people *must* open up to the prophetic, or they can be frustrated in their prayers. So what helps show us if our prayers are not God-breathed faith prayers? A prophetic word from the faith realm, the operation of the seer unction perceiving the root causes that hinder the manifestation of the miraculous. Don't tell me "seeing" in the spirit has no place in a healing ministry. We cannot negate or minimize the prophetic in the miraculous.

This is not to say there isn't a sovereign realm, and that there isn't a healing anointing, which isn't so much about one's level of faith—it is an act of kindness on God's behalf. Of course God loves people and reaches out to them. Not everyone has time to deal with all of their sin and doubt in a life-threatening situation. So don't take the above as the end-all, be-all reason for why or why not a person is healed. It is just one element to consider. Never forget, also, that God is sovereign.

"And God wrought special miracles by the hands of Paul: so that from his body were brought unto the sick handkerchiefs or aprons, and the diseases departed from them, and the evil spirits went out of them" (Acts 19:11-12 KJV). That's a sovereign act of releasing the healing anointing. Reference Acts 5:11-16, and of course, Acts 10:38 for more about the anointing.

But with all that, there is a principle here I am trying to convey: the revelatory gifts, those which are implemented in panoramic operation, the words of knowledge, the words of wisdom, that ever-important discerning of spirits, prophecy (visual and vocal, including tongues and interpretation; see 1 Corinthians 12:8,10)— these are used by the Spirit to bring the realm of heaven into the promises we have in the completed work of Calvary. These prophetic gifts visualize and then actualize miracles.

The prophetic is one of the greatest keys to releasing healing, signs, wonders and miracles. Tapping into that glory realm, that prophetic/apostolic realm of God's limitless power.

Panorama can tie into prophetic intercession as well, so let's diverge for a few paragraphs and discuss a couple principles. Basically, intercession is a warfare mantle in prayer. One of an intercessor's key responsibilities is to remind the Lord of the promises and appointments yet to be fulfilled. It takes a seeing eye and listening ear to be able to divine those unfulfilled words.

> *"I have set watchmen on your walls, O Jerusalem; they shall never hold their peace day or night. You who make mention of the Lord do not keep silent, and give Him no rest till He establishes and till He makes Jerusalem a praise in the earth."* (Isaiah 62:6-7)

Further, intercessors take up a case before God on behalf of another. They are appalled by the lack of justice for someone, and they beseech the Lord for redress against the wrongs.

> *"So truth fails, and he who departs from evil makes himself a prey. Then the Lord saw it, and it displeased Him that there was no justice. He saw that there was no man, and wondered that there was no intercessor; therefore His own arm brought salvation for Him; and His own righteousness, it sustained Him."* (Isaiah 59:15-16)

Intercessors make up the hedge, build up the wall in a time of battle. They are used by God for protection of the people. It's an important role, and one not to be taken lightly. The in-depth nature of panoramic operation can add an element of foresight to this kind of protective warfare prayer.

> *"O Israel, your prophets are like foxes in the deserts. You have not gone up into the gaps to build a wall for the house*

of Israel to stand in battle on the day of the Lord." (Ezekiel 13:4-5)

Standing in the gap, making a wall, bridging a chasm, is another significant role an intercessor plays; the discernment of panoramic operation can only heighten and intensify the prayer warrior's ability to stand between God's righteous judgment and the need for mercy on the people's behalf.

> *"So I sought for a man among them who would make a wall, and stand in the gap before Me on behalf of the land, that I should not destroy it; but I found no one. Therefore I have poured out My indignation on them; I have consumed them with the fire of My wrath; and I have recompensed their deeds on their own heads,' says the Lord God."* (Ezekiel 22:30-31)

What all this is saying is that an intercessor is the unification of the prophet and the priest. The priest pleaded the needs of the people before the Lord; the prophet pleaded the interests of God before the people.

> *"But if they are prophets, and if the word of the Lord is with them, let them now make intercession to the Lord of hosts, that the vessels which are left in the house of the Lord, in the house of the king of Judah, and at Jerusalem, do not go to Babylon."* (Jeremiah 27:18)

Prophetic intercession is assisted by panoramic discernment by amplifying the ability to receive an immediate prayer request from the Lord and coupling the prayer with divinely inspired utterance that releases the power of God in the particular situation. Can an intercessor be effective without panorama? Of course. But what we're saying here is that adding the element of panorama to one's intercession can only increase the effectiveness of their warfare, "for the weapons of our warfare are not carnal but mighty in God for pulling down strongholds..." (2 Corinthians 10:4).

Panorama also assists the intercessor in discerning and waiting before the Lord in order to hear, see and receive God's burden, (that is, His words, concerns, warnings, conditions, promises, visions, what have you) and to respond back to the Lord with the appropriate action, bringing the people to an understanding of how they should respond in turn.

The sharp intercessor would be wise not to neglect the benefit of developing a panoramic unction to their prayers.

So how do we develop this operation? How do we honor the anointing, and thus unveil the blinded eyes to the unseen realm? Our ability to see is directly connected to our understanding (again, Ephesians 1:18).

One element we must overcome is discouragement. We cannot lose the knowledge of what He has done for us in the past. Often people don't see because they don't remember. They have lost sight not only of what He did, but *who* He is. They become discouraged, and discouragement is a big problem, because how they see miracles taking place in the "now" is how they relate to what they saw *yesterday*, if that makes sense. Their past reactions to the miraculous (or a lack of the miraculous) affect the future reactions (or lack thereof) to the miraculous. Take a moment to read over these sentences again to make sure you understand what I mean.

In other words, they forget what they have seen in the past, and it makes them wary of what they will (or will not) see in the future. Let us never forget the inherent power of a testimony. What has been shared before still matters for today.

> *"And they reasoned among themselves, saying, 'It is because we have no bread.' But Jesus, being aware of it, said to*

them, 'Why do you reason because you have no bread? Do you not yet perceive nor understand? Is your heart still hardened? Having eyes, do you not see? And having ears, do you not hear? And do you not remember? When I broke the five loaves for the five thousand, how many baskets full of fragments did you take up?' They said to Him, 'Twelve.' 'Also, when I broke the seven for the four thousand, how many large baskets full of fragments did you take up?' And they said, 'Seven.' So He said to them, 'How is it you do not understand?'" (Mark 8:16-21)

Another element to overcome so that our spiritual sight can be further developed is the hardening of our hearts. The day-to-day grind of our lives serves as a process of becoming callous toward seeing the Father as Jesus saw Him. Those calluses become veils over our eyes. "And the cares of this world, the deceitfulness of riches, and the desires for other things entering in choke the word, and it becomes unfruitful" (Mark 4:19).

But, "the Holy Spirit says: 'Today if you will hear His voice, do not harden your hearts, as in the rebellion, in the day of trial in the wilderness...'" (Hebrews 3:7-8). We cannot forget that every day is today. Think about it.

Now just a little later in Hebrews 3 (Verses 12-18) we see the author showing the cause for the hardening of the heart: sin. Sin brings forth condemnation, and condemnation begets an isolation from the Lord. Isolation destroys confidence in God. (For greater teaching on overcoming isolation, refer to *The Dancing Hand of God*.)

"And by this we know that we are of the truth, and shall assure our hearts before Him. For if our heart condemns us, God is greater than our heart, and knows all things. Beloved, if our heart does not condemn us, we have

confidence toward God. And whatever we ask we receive from Him, because we keep His commandments and do those things that are pleasing in His sight." (1 John 3:19-22)

What's this passage saying? Our "heart" is in the lower, soulish realm. But God is greater—His is a higher, supernatural realm. So if our heart is not condemning us, it is because we've come up higher in His realm. How do we keep ourselves in that higher realm? By doing the things that are pleasing in His sight!

Another key to developing the seeing ability is to throw off dullness (see Hebrews 5:11,14). This is the "leaven of the Pharisees" Christ was warning against in Matthew 16:11-12. Dullness is simply the inability to hear the Spirit clearly. Those spiritual senses that discern what the Spirit is saying are muffled and dense. It is only by faith that those senses are accessed and finely tuned. What is heard must be mixed with faith to be sharply understood (see Hebrews 4:2).

Just as Jesus' conversation with Nicodemus shows in John 3:1-6, unless dullness is cast off, unless one is born of water and Spirit, unless one discerns the spiritual new birth, as Nicodemus struggled to do in his dullness, one cannot *see* the kingdom of heaven.

There must come an understanding, a spiritual perception within the life of the believer, wherein he/she hears and knows the Spirit saying to them, "I am now a Spirit living in heaven as well as abiding in you." They must be made to understand that deity actually resides in their bodies. If they truly *knew* that, really comprehended the vastness of that certainty, if they spiritually *saw* the kingdom of heaven residing in them, the miraculous expression they were looking for would flow as easily as water. Thus, the seer operation is so vital to the miraculous.

As these things are overcome: dullness, isolation, hardening and discouragement, there must be something put in their place.

To develop a discerning heart (inner knowing), a hearing ear (inner hearing), a seeing eye (inner seeing), takes the equipping of the saints. To equip them means to put things in them to mature them, season them, temper them, *perfect* them, as Ephesians 4:8-16 shows. It's raising children into mature adults. The apostle breaks into the lost, the evangelist brings in the lost. It is the prophetic and the pastoral/teaching elements of the gifts Christ gave that teach and perfect and mature.

(Yes, all five-fold are equippers, but specifically, it is prophets and pastors that temper the saints in the churches, bringing forth mature Christians. This is why the prophetic and pastoral must be linked... this is often not the case in many churches, and we are left with thousands of infantile Christians who are never fully equipped in the fashion God intended them to be. I say this in love but without pulling punches. There are, of course, many exceptions, but search your gut, listen to the Spirit, and I believe you will come to the same conclusion as me, 'cause I believe I am correct. Here we insert one of those smiley face emoticons.)

Hearing from God on how to proceed comes through the prophets. Implementing the plan to proceed comes through the pastors. They are equally vital, on the same plane of importance and preeminence, not one above the other. In fact, the prophetic (along with the apostolic) is the foundation; that is, the *floorboard* of this equipping plan Jesus has instituted in His church. If an apostle or a prophet is not acting like the underpinning, the stepping stone, then they are not acting as they should. Something to consider, for us servant-leaders.

The prophet and the pastor help the saints to confirm the inner witness; they help the sheep hear the voice of the Lord by encouraging them to listen to Him. It takes a couple of voices to get the correct interpretation on any matter (see 2 Corinthians 13:1). The two together turn the people into Stephens, *full* of faith, power, wisdom (see Acts 6:5-10)—that is the spirit of might and counsel Isaiah was talking about (again, Isaiah 11:1-2). We need *fullness* flowing in the many-membered (I don't think that's a word) body of Christ.

This cultivated inner witness of the Spirit is a mark of maturity, showing that the sheep can exercise their spiritual senses as Daniel in Chapter 7. Their imaginations are purified, rarified, submitting to God, who moves upon their minds, and enlightens their understanding (once again, Ephesians 1:18, which you should have memorized by now).

The pastors and prophets have so properly instructed and equipped the saints that they are able to use their spiritual faculties of perception to distinguish both good and evil, what is spiritual, what is soulish. The two offices have begun the process of walking through that breaking in the flock's lives, where the soulish bondage is being smashed and the Spirit is pouring through (again, as in Hebrews 4:12). These people are ready to eat strong meat.

> *"But solid food belongs to those who are of full age, that is, those who by reason of use have their senses exercised to discern both good and evil."* (Hebrews 5:14)

By reason of use have their senses exercised... The spiritual muscles must be used, there must be resistance as in physical weightlifting, so the big guns can bulk up. Christians of mature faith are those whose faculties of spiritual understanding have been carefully trained by constant practice, which makes perfect. The inner witness, how God leads His people, is sharpened and honed, taut and rippling, a solid muscle, not a flabby, wet noodle. (Take a moment to read 1 Samuel 3:6-12.)

The new creation, when we are born again, has spiritual senses, just like the natural body: spiritual eyes, ears, nose, mouth, etc. (see 1 Corinthians 15:46). These must be sharpened up, and the prophetic and pastoral giftings do just that. These offices ask these questions of the people: are your ears hearing? Are your eyes seeing? Have you been anointed? (See Revelation 3:18.) Is your inner witness being developed, that feeling, that more deeper *knowing* of what rings true in your spirit? They teach the people that the inner witness proceeds from the realm of spiritual knowledge.

> *"Behold, You desire truth in the inward parts, and in the hidden part You will make me to know wisdom."* (Psalm 51:6)

It is true that the reborn spirit is graced with spiritual sensory organs, but eyes cannot see where no light has been shined, and ears cannot hear where no sound has been made. The seeing, hearing, and knowing we perceive in the spiritual realm are of themselves based on the light and the truth given to us from the Father, and worked out through the five-fold, specifically the prophetic and pastoral operating in perfect unison together.

> *"Create in me a clean heart, O God, and renew a steadfast spirit within me."* (Psalm 51:10)

> *"...And it is the Spirit who bears witness, because the Spirit is truth."* (1 John 5:6)

The Holy Spirit, who is light, bears witness to the truth by showing our purposes, our desires and leading us into them. So in this manner, we might say God leads His people by light and truth. And I bet you Old Testament buffs can see where I'm going with this now, huh?

> *"And you shall put in the breastplate of judgment the Urim and the Thummim, and they shall be over Aaron's heart when he goes in before the Lord. So Aaron shall bear the judgment of the children of Israel over his heart before the Lord continually."* (Exodus 28:30)

*"And the governor said to them that they should not eat
of the most holy things till a priest could consult with the
Urim and Thummim."* (Nehemiah 7:65)

In the Old Testament way of things, God communicated with
the high priest when he went into the tabernacle. The priest would
don the breastplate of light and truth (*Urim* and *Thummim*) and
inquire of the Lord. *Urim* is pronounced "oo-reem," and *Thummim*
is pronounced "toom-meem"—more or less; I'm sure an Hebraic
scholar will argue with me, and they'd probably prove themselves
correct. The literal meanings are "the Lights and the Perfections."
Compare this Old Testament breastplate of judgment with the New
Testament spiritual breastplate of righteousness found in Ephesians
6:14, and we'll come full-360 in a bit.

When an OT high priest went to ask counsel of the Lord, they
wore this breastplate set with twelve stones, representing the twelve
tribes of Israel, and behind it, next to the heart, a sacred pouch
contained the special stones, *Urim* and *Thummim*. We're not exactly
sure how these stones communicated God's counsel to the priest.
The obvious implication, based on their names, is the priest would
ask a Yes or No kind of question: "should we smite one of the –ites?"
And the stones glowed warm for "yes, do smite," or cold for "no,
smite not," something along those lines. It was impossible to "miss
it," because either it glowed and was warm, or it wasn't. Simple, but
it worked.

Yet it was a foreshadowing. The stones gave way to the perfection of wood, that is the cross, and we no longer need stones telling
us who is about to get smote, or is that smitten? The point is, we're
no longer supposed to be smiting *anyone*, and our communication
is more in depth with a living God directly, than through imper-
sonal stones.

Urim (Strong's #224; it's actually transliterated *'uwriym*, but who in the English-speaking world can say that?) is the Hebrew plural for "lights," coming from the singular *'uwr* (Strong's #217; who knows how that's pronounced, ask a Klingon) for "flame, light of fire," and is representative of the Spirit. The concept to covey here is the sunrise, the break of day, one who sees light come. Also remember, at night, their light in the OT came from fire. We could say *Urim* means something akin "to give or show light, to enlighten, to shine or to set on fire."

Thummim (Strong's #8550, transliterated *tummiym*, probably from those people that make the fancy, expensive luggage, Tumi) is again Hebrew plural meaning, "perfection, perfections." The singular is *tom* (Strong's #8537, finally an easy word), and it means "integrity, completeness, fullness, innocence, simplicity."

We could correlate the Lights and the Perfections to the supreme fire and truth (the Spirit and the Word). The Spirit is often referred to as an unquenchable flame, right? As you know, or should know, the Bible is the canon of scripture and is perfect in completeness; it is the printed representation of the second Person in the Godhead, Jesus Christ the Living Word. The two together reveal the Lord God Supreme, *Elohim*, the one God in three Persons (not three gods). And *Elohim* conveys the "greatness" of God—His glory, His power, His limitless *chabod*.

Now here's something very cool. Reference Luke 24 when the risen Christ, the sum expression of all lights and perfections, fire and truth, the reason *Urim* and *Thummim* were foreshadows, opened the disciples understanding to comprehend the scriptures (see Verse 45). Note what they say in Verse 32: "Did not our heart burn within us while He talked with us on the road, and while He opened the Scriptures to us?" The disciples on the road to Emmaus had the Lights and Perfections of Jesus emblazoned in their hearts. They had on the spiritual breastplate of righteousness: the fire

(Holy Spirit in salvation) made the truth (the Word) understandable. How astounding! Who's that cook that goes, "Bam!" I need him to say that here.

Okay, nifty. How do we apply this to developing a hearing ear and a seeing eye? Whenever a believer (who is a priest by virtue of the New Covenant) goes in to inquire of the Lord, they may expect to receive the witness of the Holy Spirit to their spirit. If they wait upon the Lord until their own will is submitted to His will, the Spirit will bear witness to the truth of God in their spirit, and they will know the will of the Lord in the particular situation they are praying for. All of this is based on their understanding of how the Lord operates.

To develop a panoramic operation, a seer gifting, one of the driving motivations must to be to posess a discerning spirit. There must also be that unquenchable passion to mature the life of the Christian and develop the kind of character that permits the reputation of God, the miraculous power of His glory, to rest upon the person. It's what those who hold the applause of heaven are looking for.

YEMEN

W E WERE BLESSED TO BE a part of a forerunning trip to Yemen, a country of nearly twenty-five million Muslims, and about 3,000 Christians. (That's called a *minority*...) We were aware of about 120-150 of them—just wonderful, fine people who were dedicated to an extremely difficult part of the Middle Eastern world grasped in the stranglehold of Islam. It's a backward country (only about half the population is literate) with a difficult terrain of deserts and rugged mountains. And it's *hot* in Yemen.

So we were in a public conference setting, which was technically illegal, but we held it anyway. There were quite a number of Muslims mixed in with this handful of Christians, to whom I was preaching about kingdom principles. We were trying to help equip them for reaching their Muslim neighbors. Most of the Christians were in agreement with what was being shared, but a few were very resistant. Not to be demeaning, I wasn't really having problems with the Muslims, but rather a small group of unbelieving believers. Now, in their defense, they were pretty much a beaten down group—imagine trying to share your faith when you're outnumbered, like, 8,000 to 1.

But that doesn't negate the truth of the kingdom. A mark of maturity for the believer is a lack of intimidation, a spirit of boldness that is attractive to the world at large. These were great people, but perhaps a little stunted. For them, the nature of the kingdom was to be a disciple personally, not make *more* disciples. And while I commend anyone who strives for a holy lifestyle, it is also the *demonstration* of that holy lifestyle, combined with signs, wonders and miracles, that creates in others a desire to become disciples as well. A disciple is, yes, a person of character and maturity, but a disciple is also one who *practices* their discipline, makes it stand for something to the rest of the world.

I was sort of upbraiding them in love, and it was kind of confrontational, so some were bristling at what I was conveying. I was saying things like, "You know, some of you have been Christian missionaries for twenty-five years here, and there's been no progression evangelistically whatsoever." I know that's easier to say for an American where you're *not* arrested for sharing your faith in your home country, but there still needs to be a boldness among the Christians, no matter how few they are, no matter where they are.

I was telling them you cannot advance the kingdom of God with just words only—there must be a display of power behind it. I only believe in power evangelism. It's a very clear-cut concept: stand up, proclaim there is only one God named Jesus, all other gods (insert whichever false deity you're combating here) are bogus, and to prove it to you, bring up your sick and He'll heal them. Simple. Effective.

But this concept was foreign to a lot of those dear Yemeni missionaries, *ergo, la résistance.* (I think I just mixed Latin and French, *verdad?*)

This went on until a Muslim man stood in front of me with a right arm that had not grown correctly. Here was a man, I guess, about thirty-five with a shriveled, emaciated arm roughly the size of a five-year-old boy's, just dangling uselessly. I remember placing my hand on his right shoulder, and I saw the panorama unfold. I could still see the small arm, but it was like I saw the outline of the full, correctly-sized arm just how God wanted it to be, the shoulder, the biceps, the elbow, the forearm, the wrist. This vision came from my internal thoughts, not outward, and was superimposed in my eyesight over the shrunken arm.

As I placed my hand on his shoulder, it sounded like popcorn, which may strike you as a little gross; but there was this *pop*, *pop*, *pop*, and the shoulder grew to its proper size. What's wild is, the physical shoulder filled out until it touched the lines of the superimposed panoramic arm I was seeing—and yes, God stayed within the lines...

The same thing happened when I put my hand on his wrist. It filled out to the line of the panoramic arm—the hand, the forearm, the elbow, and the biceps, up to the shoulder. The whole process took, I don't know, maybe two, three minutes. That's what I call a creative miracle—but it was panoramic, too. See how it blends together?

The man started to sob, and it created such a stir of amazement that he asked us, "Would you please come to my village? It's not too far from here. We have some people you could minister to." Keep in mind this guy was Muslim.

So we went with him, and the team pulled out just about every person with a crippling condition they could find, children with polio, men and women with deformities, what have you. To the best of my knowledge, they saw 100 percent success. I was led to a couple homes where the men inside were completely demonized and had to be isolated from the population. In one case, the dude was so violent, he was chained to a wall. That was creepy! But God was merciful and drove out the demons in them all. Praise His name!

During the course of this trip, I prophesied that in three to four years, there would be a move of God's Spirit that would begin to change the cultural mindset of the Yemeni people. I learned a couple years later, that a group of about thirty of these missionaries rallied around wanting to see this open-heavens expression in their country. They established harp and bowl ministry, and when the news of all the crippled villagers being healed started trickling out, they went to other villages, seeing tremendous results. At one point in time, I was told the group was composed of dozens and dozens of these firebrands, and they were all going out into the villages with signs, wonders and miracles following after them.

When I was in England, I met with some of them, and they told me that one of the initial reasons for the upheavals there was because all of the miracles the people were seeing were being translated into wanting that kind of freedom in the rest of their lives. Now, I know there are many reasons for the protests in Yemen; but praise God, these people were persuaded one of the main flashpoints for the demonstrations originated because of the release of the miraculous. Not that the people themselves necessarily knew of the miracles, but that spiritually those miracles did a special work (see Acts 19:11) in pulling down the strongholds of repression, and in the natural, it was translated culturally into the people getting a taste for wanting the kind of freedoms the kingdom offers.

And all from the establishment of panoramic, prophetic declaration! Makes you wanna shout, huh? Go ahead. No one can hear you.

THE CHARACTER OF
THE PANORAMIC SEER

O NE OF THE MARKS OF a mature child of God is the ability to be led by the Spirit, to perceive His operation in their life and the lives of those they come in contact with. The mature, full-grown sons (and daughters—it's a term not intended to be gender-specific, just as men are also the Bride of Christ; see Galatians 3:28) of God are capable of reproducing the Father's influence in their own lives and then become fathers (and mothers) themselves, reproducing others, going into all the world and making disciples (see Matthew 28:19).

The Greek word for "son" is *huios* (Strong's #5207); it means someone who shares the same nature as their Father, having more and more developed an identical character, since they have a legal right to make claim to inheriting their Father's nature. Neat, huh?

Maturity in the Christian's life is a main principle of this kingdom invasion that is such a popular subject right now, what I might term "earthing the glory." (Hey, that'd be a great title for a book…

hint, hint. Don't steal it, it's copyrighted.) As we discussed in the last section, maturity is the ability to use one's spiritual faculties of perception to distinguish between good and evil, the soulish and the spiritual; that is the solid food those of mature faith, trained by practice, are to consume.

> *"And all Israel from Dan to Beersheba knew that Samuel had been established as a prophet of the Lord. Then the Lord appeared again in Shiloh. For the Lord revealed Himself to Samuel in Shiloh by the word of the Lord."* (1 Samuel 3:20-21)

Samuel the Seer is a prime example of one who through constant practice had his spiritual faculties carefully trained to be led by the Spirit. The word of the Lord came to Samuel, and he was able to discern it, to perceive it was from Him. He had repeated experiences, encounters, with the Lord. He was able to look up and to *see*.

> *"And shall make him of quick understanding in the fear of the Lord: and he shall not judge after the sight of his eyes, neither reprove after the hearing of his ears..."* (Isaiah 11:3, KJV)

That "quick understanding" is the developed ability of translating the language of the Spirit in the fear of the Lord. A mature Christian is one who has developed their ability to express their intuitiveness to the Holy Spirit through their five senses. In other words, what is being experienced inwardly is expressed outwardly, and it affects others around them. That is the nature of panoramic operation, the nature of one who has garnered the applause of heaven.

The language of the Spirit may be spiritual intuition; that is, the language of knowing, inwardly. We discussed this quite a bit previously. But the Spirit can also speak by physical leadings; that is, the language of physical sensations—the Word being made flesh, as it were (see John 1:14). This is what Paul meant in 2 Corinthians 3:2. We become the living epistles, known and read by all men. Our very lifestyles, our characters, create a perception of the Lord to others. Mature sons and daughters of God must understand this.

Dreams are also the language of the Spirit, the language of emotions, of the heart and of the passion. Visions are the language of images, and audible leadings are the language of the spoken word of God, including prophecies. That's a lot to have to develop in order to be able to translate the language of the Spirit correctly to others.

But that is the "hope of our calling" that the oft-quoted Ephesians 1:18 verse is speaking of. As a Christian of mature character, in the context we are discussing, wherever you go, you can establish the rule of the kingdom.

> *"…And raised us up together, and made us sit together in the heavenly places in Christ Jesus…"* (Ephesians 2:6)

That short verse has a very powerful application. "Raised us up together" is the Greek word *synegeiro* (Strong's #4891), where you will probably recognize the English word "synergy," meaning "energy together" in its most simplistic definition, like symphony means "sound together." "Made us sit together" is *sygkathizo* (Strong's #4776; the Greek's worse than the Hebrew!). *Syg* is *syn*; trust me, it is. Look it up. And *kathizo* means "to appoint, confer a kingdom, to have one's abode fixed, settled down."

All of that shows the blending, the union, of our calling with Christ Jesus that is the expression of the kingdom conveyed to the world in a synergistic display of His power through us. Now that's two pretty potent paragraphs gleaned from seventeen words of scripture. Not bad.

The point is, heaven's influence in your life needs to invade this earth realm; that is earthing the glory©: the third heaven is to be experienced in the first heaven, since we are seated with Him in heavenly places, positionally sharing a kingdom with Him. Hallelujah!

As always, Jesus provides the perfect illustration, and since He is the key to His own ministry being shared with us, I'll take a moment to outline a bit about it, if you don't mind. And I'm sure you don't…

At Christ's baptism, the heavens were opened to Him, and He took open heavens with Him wherever He went. Like I've said before, He went around handing out heaven. How remarkable is that!

> *"And He said to him, 'Most assuredly, I say to you, hereafter you shall see heaven open, and the angels of God ascending and descending upon the Son of Man.'"* (John 1:51)

> *"No one has ascended to heaven but He who came down from heaven, that is, the Son of Man who is in heaven."* (John 3:13)

Keep in mind Jesus made that last statement while He was standing on earth, thus implying He was in heaven while standing on earth. And He called Himself the Son of Man, His term for showing His utter manness—not Godness—(those are totally made-up words), so we can't wimp out and say He was referring to Himself as omnipresent deity. No, as fully Man, He was standing on this earth in one spot and claimed to be in heaven at the same time. Why? Because the heavens were opened to Him. Heaven was like a cloud that came down and encircled Jesus. The Lord spoke, healed and ministered entirely under that cloud of heaven. That is why Jesus was able to say He "saw" the Father in John 5:19.

"And I heard a loud voice from heaven saying, 'Behold, the tabernacle of God is with men, and He will dwell with them, and they shall be His people. God Himself will be with them and be their God'" (Revelation 21:3). How can we neglect so great a salvation as that? (see Hebrews 2:3-4).

Take a look at Acts 8:1-8. Here's Saul fiercely persecuting the church after Stephen's murder, and the Christians are scattered, but it doesn't have the effect the religious zealot intended, does it? For now instead of having a concentrated mess to deal with, Saul has an explosive mess to deal with. And we see Philip slipping down to Samaria and preaching Christ to them. And the multitudes believe what he tells them. Why? Because they hear and see the miracles he did.

That hearing and seeing is the commodity of heaven being released to the world at large—the miraculous being displayed. And the religious spirits do not want the kingdom to be heard, seen or felt out in the world (perhaps they don't so much mind in the tabernacle, because that's relatively safe). But they don't want you to become a sign and wonder, a living epistle, to the world. Why? Because what is the byproduct of that commodity being doled out to the world? "Great joy!" (Acts 8:8).

Great joy is what happens when people are delivered of a spirit of divination, that imitation of the divine which panorama is so adept at discerning and casting out. That's why the very next verse, Acts 8:9, goes right into talking about Simon the Sorcerer. That "astonishment" is a bewitching, being ensorcelled, smitten with a glaze of indifference toward the moving of God, a mirage, a stronghold, a spirit of stupor. It doesn't want the people to exercise their spiritual intuitiveness, because then it would be found out! It tries to hold its dominion of spiritual dullness over the people. It seduces them to remain shallow. It sentences them to limitation. It wants them to stay down, stay under, stay dull, where there is no true freedom, having *words* but no *power*, no healing... no deliverance! "...having a form of godliness but denying its power. And from such people turn away!" (2 Timothy 3:5). In short, having no joy. I don't know about you, but I will not be intimidated! I will come up, come out from under, become sharp.

I have said it before: the greatest intimidation in being used by God is that you won't have what you are in need of at the time of ministry. And it is a lie. We have access, acceptance as one of the beloved. "For through Him we both have access by one Spirit to the Father... in whom we have boldness and access with confidence through faith in Him" (Ephesians 2:18; 3:12). It is the mark of a mature son or daughter of God to be able to know this and make it actual, to cause the people around us to feel, to see, to hear God physically, for Him to be enlarged and magnified. He becomes so large and so real to the people, it shatters the falsity of divination out there in the world. That is the reward of the prophetic mixing with the miraculous: it awakens the people's spiritual senses.

> *"Then Moses said to him, 'Are you zealous for my sake? Oh, that all the Lord's people were prophets and that the Lord would put His Spirit upon them!'"* (Numbers 11:29)

Moses' wish was correct. To a certain extent, all of us as mature Christians need to be prophetic (having a discerning heart, a hearing ear and a seeing eye) even if we're not all "prophets" in the Ephesians 4:11 sense. The church's foundation is built upon apostles and prophets, with Jesus as the cornerstone (see Ephesians 2:20). But it is not enough to be prophetic, there must be character established in a prophetic person; that is what this book is trying to show. This is how we are "to make our calling and election sure" (2 Peter 1:10).

The principle is this: as mature Christians we are to be a people of such firm conviction that nothing can sway us from a *heart of integrity* to fulfill a task in honesty and veracity. We are to be fashioned into faithful messengers of God's word and power, for "a wicked messenger falls into trouble, but a faithful ambassador brings health" (Proverbs 13:17). Take a moment to study Jeremiah 15:15-21, especially Verse 19.

In that verse, the word "precious" is *yaqar* (Strong's #3368), and it means "bright, clear, rare, honorable, weighty, noble, important, valuable, prized, splendid, costly, glorious, influential, jewels." Conversely "vile" is *zalal* (Strong's #2151), meaning "worthless, insignificant, thought of lightly, shake as in the wind, tremble, quake, loose of morals." If we can take the *yaqar* from out the *zalal*, we can be the mouth of God. Truth must be given in the character and personality of Jesus; it is a requirement to teach, preach and prophesy as Jesus would have, in His integrity of character, for the truth, power, glory to be manifested such that attracts the applause of heaven. Only those "shall stand before [Him]" (Jeremiah 15:19).

It is possible to speak the truth in a wrong spirit, and thus neglect the Spirit behind the letter. To avoid such travesty, the panoramic seer must feel the burden of *God* not just the burden of the message. The character exemplified becomes the expression of the message itself, revealing more than just the word, but the power behind it. Prophets represent God in their speech and actions, not just the message God has given them. As such, modern mature prophets deal with heart issues, and rarely (not *never*) address the world's issues, but primarily the church's issues.

The travesty of truth spoken in the wrong spirit, a shallow spirit, is such that it produces no lasting fruit, it brings about no permanent changes, in the lives of the listeners. It's a feel-good moment that quickly passes the people by. It's a good sermon, not a life-changing encounter. While it's important to be accurate as a prophet, it is equally important to bring repentance, to break through the divination, to shatter misconceptions about God that hinder His flow of power and glory. Otherwise, we are giving words with specific information, but no substance, and that is appallingly sad. Because the revelation of an empty, vile word, with no precious worth, may stop the listener from outwardly sinning, but it brings no repentance, no work of grace, no true heart change. And as we pointed out early on in this book, a lack of repentance brings trouble and judgment to the listener, a distinct lack of joy. In short, worthless words desolate the people.

> *"Many rulers [shepherd, pastors] have destroyed My vineyard, they have trodden My portion underfoot; they have made My pleasant portion a desolate wilderness. They have made it desolate; desolate, it mourns to Me; the whole land is made desolate, because no one takes it to heart."* (Jeremiah 12:10-11)

But don't lose heart. The Lord promises: "And I will give you shepherds according to My heart, who will feed you with knowledge and understanding" (Jeremiah 3:15).

If your heart as a prophetic person is broken—it brings brokenness to others. It's a highly translatable substance. Truth must bear fruit in your life as a panoramic seer; you have a choice to be a healer or a trouble maker. And I'm sure we all know some prophets out there who are trouble makers. Where's their fruit?

> *"Who build up Zion with bloodshed and Jerusalem with iniquity: her heads judge for a bribe, her priests teach for pay, and her prophets divine for money. Yet they lean on the Lord, and say, 'Is not the Lord among us? No harm can come upon us.'"* (Micah 3:10-11)

We're not only to be faithful messengers, but pure messengers. Undiluted, not able to be bought. Take a few minutes to study Ezekiel 13:1-10. Impure prophets, that is, those with a lack of character, speak out of their own folly, negate their burden, and toss off the pressing of God. They refuse to go up into the gap, to identify the sin, to recognize the breach in the wall. A pure messenger, one of character, is not only willing, but desirous, to stand in the gap—a place where they stand *alone*, because no one else wants the position, or perhaps no one else is anointed for the position. In either case, be pure, be willing to stand alone, use tempered mortar to repair the wall.

Impure prophets don't make up the hedge, see? They pull their shoulders back from the grind wheel of discipline. "But they refused to heed, shrugged their shoulders, and stopped their ears so that they could not hear" (Zechariah 7:11). They don't wait upon the Lord for the answer someone is seeking. They're loathe to position themselves to help release the answer for the people, but they seduce people with flattering words, which in turn, makes them (the prophets) vain. Their priorities are all mixed up; they're self-centered. Don't be this kind of prophet! Have better character!

That bit about plastering the wall with untempered mortar (see Ezekiel 13:10) means the impure prophets are untested; they leave holes in the walls of the church; they have no understanding of battle strategies; they offer no protection. The mixture makes them weak, effeminate, soft. They rely on stock phrases, the normal answers to the questions people bring them, with no fire mixed with it. They cry, "Peace," when the world is burning. Again, don't be this kind of prophet!

> *"Cursed is he who does the work of the Lord deceitfully, and cursed is he who keeps back his sword from blood. Moab has been at ease from his youth; he has settled on his dregs, and has not been emptied from vessel to vessel, nor has he gone into captivity. Therefore his taste remained in him, and his scent has not changed."* (Jeremiah 48:10-11)

Ultimately these kinds of prophets of weak character do the work of the Lord deceitfully; they end up working for personal gain, for vainglory's sake. There is never any change in their lives because they don't yield to the prunings, dealings, of the Lord. The cycles of life are broken. By that I mean, we all go through cycles wherein we change and then yield to the next level of change as the Spirit deals with us. But impure prophets stay stagnated; they are never poured from vessel to vessel and become settled on their dregs, turning fetid. Their scent has not changed. They end up stinking.

I'd call this the Moab spirit: any person who desires the gifting of God without the preparations. Notice Moab was "at ease" from his youth—lazy, lethargic, self-indulgent and self-centered. I believe there is a Moab spirit in the church, but God is sending "filters," so to speak. Those of us who will separate the liquid from the dregs. Those who will fill in the breaches of the church's wall with tempered, fire-tested mortar that comes from the crushings of the Spirit, the gold refined in fire according to Revelation 3:18. We will be the watchmen on the walls of Isaiah 62, never keeping silent until the wall and the city are rebuilt.

> *"The prophets prophesy falsely, and the priests rule by their own power; and My people love to have it so. But what will you do in the end?"* (Jeremiah 5:31)

Once again, and say it with me, once more with feeling: don't be this kind of prophet. We are "partakers of the divine nature" (2 Peter 1:4)! My first book went to great lengths on the back and forth of separating the holy from the profane, the clean and the unclean (see Ezekiel 44:23-24), so I'll spare the reader from repeating it here, but the principle remains. Can't get away from it! Otherwise:

> *"So I will break down the wall you have plastered with untempered mortar, and bring it down to the ground, so that its foundation will be uncovered; it will fall, and you shall be consumed in the midst of it. Then you shall know that I am the Lord."* (Ezekiel 13:14)

FOLLOWING LOVE

THE PURPOSE OF PANORAMIC OPERATION is to set people free, to administer the anointing that shatters whatever yoke or oppression they may be under: usually that's a physical healing need. This is why the vast majority of Christ's ministry was healings, because most people have some kind of need for healing in their bodies. Now often an underlying mental or emotional oppression is a root cause of whatever physical ailment a person has, so it's not a blanket statement; but in its simplest capacity, this type of operation is for bringing healing to a person.

> *"And I fell at his feet to worship him. But he said to me, 'See that you do not do that! I am your fellow servant, and of your brethren who have the testimony of Jesus. Worship God! For the testimony of Jesus is the spirit of prophecy."* (Revelation 19:10)

What does that mean? The testimony of Jesus is the spirit of prophecy? What Jesus did on this earth—that is, signs, wonders, miracles, raising the dead, cleansing the sick, healing the lepers— these activities are an invitation for us to experience and repeat the exact same operations in our lives. It's really quite simple. Jesus didn't make it very hard, because He recognized most people needed healing, and it was a perfect way to witness to them of His forgiveness and dominion over sin. He drew people to His kingdom because He healed them.

His testimony, those works He wrought to prove the validity of what He was saying about His Father in heaven, is rooted in the prophetic unction today. Part of this is found in panorama, melding the seer operation of the prophetic with healing. But the reason we are not seeing the same level of success that He did is because we need to minister under a greater heaviness of God's manifest glory. Panorama is one such type of operation in a condensed atmosphere of His *chabod*.

(Once again, I mean on an individual level in day-to-day life—I understand the Lord is healing and touching people all the time, everywhere, especially when we step back and look at things on a macro level throughout the world. But I think you would have to agree with me that a lot of times, the people who attend your church, the person standing in line at your grocery store, the man or woman you work next to at the office, who have a physical need of healing—they struggle to receive it. Or they receive it in measure. It's not a critical statement; it's just an observation.)

> *"He who receives a prophet in the name of a prophet shall receive a prophet's reward. And he who receives a righteous man in the name of a righteous man shall receive a righteous man's reward."* (Matthew 10:41)

We need to start emphasizing the importance of prophetic operation in the midst of healing needs. Part of the solution is to work on creating a habitation for God's glory, having His reputation rest on us *permanently*—where He *lives* with us corporately, not just comes down to visit from time-to-time. We don't just need revival, we need vitality.

> *"...In whom you also are being built together for a dwelling place of God in the Spirit."* (Ephesians 2:22)

So all this stuff we've been talking about has been about cultivating right motivations, breakings, character development, sensitivity, integrity, etc., so that the Lord will entrust that kind of co-habitation with us. We have to develop a corporate discerning heart, that inner knowing to perceive where the Lord is at; a hearing ear, that inner voice that guides and directs us when we see the Lord is *not* where we are; a seeing eye, inner vision, that Christ had so finely tuned to perceive the Father in heaven, and therefore, duplicate on earth what He saw Him doing.

> *"So the Lord said to Moses: 'Gather to Me seventy men of the elders of Israel, whom you know to be the elders of the people and officers over them; bring them to the tabernacle of meeting, that they may stand there with you. Then I will come down and talk with you there. I will take of the Spirit that is upon you and will put the same upon them; and they shall bear the burden of the people with you, that you may not bear it yourself alone."* (Numbers 11:16-17)

See, there's a prophetic Spirit we're supposed to be carrying here. But I'd like to suggest taking it a little further than what most of us assume a prophetic Spirit means and wed that to the miraculous. This seer operation, this panorama, is perhaps of a higher order than the simple prophecy that most of us recognize—the corporate prophecy, or presbytery, or personal prophecy for edification, exhortation and comfort. Now, higher order doesn't mean "better" as if the other levels of prophecy are somehow inferior. Each has their place in the body of Christ, and since the 1980s we've seen restoration of the prophetic as we know it; but this concept of panoramic seer operation that breeds the miraculous is still primarily underplayed.

Just as we need to wed discerning of spirits and a gift of faith to our ministry operations to see a greater release of the miraculous, we must also wed the prophetic into the healing anointing.

Look, all any minister of the Lord can do is stand there with the person in need and *initiate an encounter with God* by His wisdom and direction. That's all. We can bind and loose, and pray and fast, and Jericho march and weep (all wonderful, all have their place)— but ultimately, the only way the people are going to get healed, saved and delivered is if we say, hold hands with me and let's meet God. I sometimes think we make it too difficult. It's actually not a hard concept to grasp—initiate an encounter and let the people meet Him—but it's the *application* that can seem complicated, the implementation that requires something a little deeper than just "holding hands."

We as ministers, in whatever capacity we serve, need to be standing in the counsel of God. What does that mean, counsel of God? It is the working of the Holy Spirit in giving insight, advice and plans that will release a demonstration of mighty acts of His power. This is the "key of the house of David" in Isaiah 22:22-23 and Revelation 3:7. For us, it is knowing and perceiving the unseen realm and entering into heaven's influence to bind and loose, releasing the very activity of God among the people while tripping up the works and strategy of the enemy.

We are to be messengers sent by Him with a mantle of counsel and might (again, Isaiah 11:2). "Might" is a pretty good word. The Hebrew is *gebuwrah* (Strong's #1369); the Greek is *kratos* (Strong's #2904; Ephesians 6:10), and we might could say it is the revelation of the muscularity of God behind the power He wields, the limitless potential for energy. That is to say, it's not just the display of power (*dunamis*, Strong's #1411), but the underlying support *behind* the power. Make a fist—that is the support behind the power. Now strike with that fist (don't hurt yourself)—that is the display of the power. The distinction is subtle, but impressive; kind of like potential energy versus kinetic energy. Remember your physics class from high school?

But with all this talk of being muscular, the question to ask is how do we release and impart that potential energy into kinetic energy; that is, how do we convert the might to power?

"Pursue love, and desire spiritual gifts, but especially that you may prophesy." (1 Corinthians 14:1)

Following after love. Did you know love has a flow, and that we can follow after it, literally walking in love? "This is love, that we walk according to His commandments. This is the commandment, that as you have heard from the beginning, you should walk in it" (2 John 6).

I want to honor my brother-in-law, David Alsobrook, for a wonderful book he has written called *Learning to Love*. It is worth your while to read it—some of the concepts discussed in this chapter were gleaned from that book, so I want to credit David here for his insight.

Romans 5:5 says, "the love of God has been poured out in our hearts by the Holy Spirit who was given to us." In the case of the leper in Mark 1, Jesus was moved with compassion. What is compassion? Focused love. It is love brought to bear upon an individual in a specific area of hurt. In this case, Jesus focused His love upon the leper's need to be free of his disease. When love is projected, grace is manifested. "And the whole multitude sought to touch Him, for power went out from Him and healed them all" (Luke 6:19).

Every human's spirit senses when love is projected, and love is the power which energizes the miracle to begin. Love is the conduit that converts the potential energy of might into the kinetic energy of *dunamis*. It must be focused, directed, moved. This is why we are told to pursue love, to become followers of love.

It is the energizing power behind the *dunamis*—that is, the power and grace of God which actually completes the miracle. It is a catalyst for releasing faith and authority. "...faith working through love" (Galatians 5:6). Faith is energized, activated, or made operational by love, and therefore, if we find no power in operation in any given need in a person's life, most likely it is due to a lack of energizing love.

I always recall one of France Metcalfe's quips to me: "How you minister to the people on earth in love is what is important to the King above."

When we are told by Paul to desire spiritual gifts, it is the only act of coveting we can commit without sin, if it is done with the right heart motivation. Why is it coveting without sin? Because we are simply coveting more of the Lord. The gifts of the Spirit is the greatness and might of God made visible, audible, tangible to the people. We do not serve some dumb idol, but a vibrant, physical God. Spiritual gifts reveal the very personage of God. They give an outlet for the fruit of the Spirit to be expressed. Thus, the two go hand in hand, and that is why it isn't wrong to covet spiritual gifts.

> *"Then He said, 'I will make all My goodness pass before you, and I will proclaim the name of the Lord before you. I will be gracious to whom I will be gracious, and I will have compassion on whom I will have compassion.'"* (Exodus 33:19)

> *"Now the Lord descended in the cloud and stood with him there, and proclaimed the name of the Lord. And the Lord*

passed before him and proclaimed, 'The Lord, the Lord
God, merciful and gracious, longsuffering, and abounding
in goodness and truth…'" (Exodus 34:5-6)

It is that goodness of the Lord that is found in spiritual gifts.
But rather that you may prophesy! Don't forget the spirit of prophecy is the testimony of Jesus. "…for prophecy never came by the will of man, but holy men of God spoke as they were moved by the Holy Spirit" (2 Peter 1:21). You probably know that word "moved" is the Greek *phero* (Strong's #5342), and it means to rush, drive forward (like a ship being driven by gale-force winds), and to bring forth or bear (a maternity term, when the baby takes its first shocking breath of life and begins to cry).

Secrets of the heart are made manifest in prophecy, revealing what is lacking or hindering in a person's life for them to receive their healing. Recall that *nabiy'* flow of the prophetic, the words bubbling forth—the free-flowing word of the Lord—that is the flow of love being vocalized for a person's "edification, exhortation and comfort" (1 Corinthians 14:3), and every one of us may learn to prophesy (see Verse 31). The gifts of the Spirit are released through the vocal chords—so speak! Be *phero*'d! Mix that spirit of prophecy with a divine flow of love yielding compassion to see the people's hurts healed. This is why developing that inner witness is so important, to be sensitive to the Lord's leading, that flow of love toward the people.

The world's people are starving—they're desperate for personal ministry, an intimate touch from the Lord, the love, nearness, and acceptance of God. They have to be shown they're not just tolerated by Him, but that they can "come boldly unto the throne of grace" (Hebrews 4:16), and He is equally available to all.

Part of one's inability to receive and, then, express love stems from a fear issue. That they will not be accepted. That they will be rejected. By initiating those love encounters with God for fearful people, we give them an opportunity to trust in the Lord. To be frank and truthful with Him.

> *"There is no fear in love; but perfect love casts out fear, because fear involves torment. But he who fears has not been made perfect in love. We love Him because He first loved us."* (1 John 4:18-19)

I've said it before, we as ministers must become sensitive to those unmet love needs in people's lives, to become touched with the feelings of those who are seeking God. He sends love messengers to meet those needs, but you can't give what you haven't received, you know?

You've probably heard it taught in John 21:15-19, the restoration of Peter to Christ, wherein Jesus asks Peter twice if he loves Him (*agapao*, Strong's #25—"dearly love," the God-kind of love, love unto death) to which Peter can only respond that he loves Him (*phileo*, Strong's #5368—to be fond of, "friendly love"). The third time Jesus asks the question, He substitutes *agapao* with *phileo* as if to say, "Peter, do you even have brotherly affection for Me?" Exasperated, Peter says, "Come on, You know I do, Lord."

See, after Peter's thrice denial of Christ, he felt unworthy to call himself *agapao* of the Lord. He needed a special acknowledgment from Jesus that he was accepted and forgiven. By telling him to "feed His sheep," the risen Lord was commissioning Peter to cultivate that kind of love for His people (*agapao*, not just *phileo*.) Now, after Peter's baptism in the Holy Spirit, that love of God was enlarged, and we all know the exploits Peter wrought. And in a strange way, Jesus comforted Peter by saying, Yes, you will *agapao* Me, don't worry, because you're going to die a martyr's death for My sake—somewhat of a bittersweet promise, huh? I don't think, when the time came, that Peter minded so much dying for the One he loved.

The point is, you and I, like Peter, must have love encounters with the Lord. And just as in the apostle's case, it is God who always takes the first step; He makes Himself available to us; He apprehends us first. And yes, our love for Him may require the ultimate sacrifice, but for those of us who have fallen in *agapao* with Him, that's all right, if need be.

Love encounters with the Lord change us, just as they changed John from a Son of Thunder (see Mark 3:17) into the Beloved (see John 13:23). But like John, we have to make ourselves available to those love encounters. We cannot change ourselves. Jesus was equally available to the other eleven, and of course they loved Him, but it was John who really took advantage of his access to the Lord. He highly esteemed and delighted in that closeness with Christ, and Jesus transformed John because of it.

Once we are changed because of those love embraces with God, we can then give out to others what we have received. We have to realize we are not the originators of love, merely the recipients of it.

"He who does not love does not know God, for God is love" (1 John 4:8). To the extent one receives and expresses love, it can be said that one knows God.

"And now abide faith, hope, love, these three; but the greatest of these is love" (1 Corinthians 13:13). "And we have known and believed the love that God has for us. God is love, and he who abides in love abides in God, and God in him" (1 John 4:16). Love abides in us, as we become sensitive to the needs of others, following that flow of love leading to compassion, we become changed into the love messengers that God uses to reach the lost and hurting.

How this ties into the prophetic, and moving in panoramic operation, is that focused love, which is compassion, is the scout that seeks out the need. It is the focal point, square one, the start, to seeing the miraculous. I'm always asked by people how I know who God wants to minister to. The answer is I follow the focusing love. I tune my inner vision to that flow of God's love, and when it focuses on a particular person, I know God wants to touch them. Compassion is kind of like a magnifying glass that concentrates the sun's rays into a distilled, burning force. I know at the end of that flow of love is a gift, a healing, a word waiting to come forth.

So it is not just important... it is *essential* in the most fundamental way to develop a sensitivity to God's flow of love toward hurting people. It is the first step, box numero uno, in energizing the miraculous. Without following after love, we might as well not even bother trying to minister to people for we will never understand their needs without focused compassion toward them, and all of our efforts to release the power of God, all of our attempts to garner the applause of heaven, are minimized at best, thwarted and abortive at worst. And the people we meet are in too much need to deal with a bunch of ministers devoid of love, so let us give them what they require!

WHY DOES GOD SIT ON A THRONE?

R IGHTEOUSNESS IS ANOTHER FACET OF release in panoramic operation that should not be overlooked. As important as following the flow of love and cultivating compassion is to releasing the miraculous melded with the prophetic, it is also our positional authority in the Lord that gives us a right to make those demands on the anointing to set people free. That's what righteousness means, right-standing, an ability as a son (and daughter)—remember *huios* (Strong's #5207)—of God to approach His throne and expect an audience with the King of all kings. It's not arrogance, anymore than you would consider it superciliousness for one of your own children to approach you, expecting you to meet their physical needs. Yes, we should never, ever, forget that it is only by God's grace we are adopted into His family; but we shouldn't, out of some false sense of piety and self-righteousness, neglect our relational standing with the Father. Remember, parents give their children good gifts (see Matthew 7:7-12), and they love doing so!

"Behold what manner of love the Father has bestowed on us, that we should be called children of God! Therefore the world does not know us, because it did not know Him." (1 John 3:1)

It is a special place in the echelon of humanity to be called a child of God. It is called the Sonship Anointing, and it is a position of authority and inheritance, providing access to Him who sits on the throne of creation. And have you ever wondered *why* God sits on a throne? Does that mean anything, or is it just something a King does? Would He be any less God if He sat under a tree? No. But the throne reveals an attribute of His Godness (I copyrighted that made-up word, so you can't use it without paying me a quarter).

"Righteousness and justice are the foundation of Your throne; mercy and truth go before Your face." (Psalm 89:14)

Justice, judgment. Mercy, truth. God sits on a throne to uphold the order of His righteousness which brings life to all His creation. Righteousness means "right-ness." Take a moment to re-read Revelation 4; let it sink in, the awesomeness of His throne. God sits on a throne because He is righteous, meaning God will *always* do right. It is right and just that He bestows a covenant of healing and health for His children. It is right and just that His people are saved and delivered. It is right and just that we have access to the power He has delegated to His sons.

It is His very character and nature to do right, because He is righteous. That sounds circular, but it is true. The Father's heart, identity and authority are rooted in His character of righteousness. His sitting on a throne means we can trust Him.

"... I saw the Lord sitting on a throne, high and lifted up, and the train of His robe filled the temple." (Isaiah 6:1)

His kingdom influence and rule stems from His righteousness, and it is inherited by His children when they come to Him through His firstborn Son. It is what has caused us to be translated into a reality of overcoming, being superior to the death and loss associated with our fallen nature. We are seated with Him positionally, experientially, because His righteousness has become our righteousness. It is what enables us to be obedient to Him, and in return, He releases His authority to His dutiful children. God's loving-kindness accompanies the release of His authority. "Mercy and truth have met together; righteousness and peace have kissed" (Psalm 85:10).

> *"'This is the covenant that I will make with them after those days,' says the Lord: 'I will put My laws into their hearts, and in their minds I will write them,' then He adds, 'Their sins and their lawless deeds I will remember no more.' Now where there is remission of these, there is no longer an offering for sin. Therefore, brethren, having boldness to enter the Holiest by the blood of Jesus, by a new and living way which He consecrated for us, through the veil, that is, His flesh, and having a High Priest over the house of God, let us draw near with a true heart in full assurance of faith, having our hearts sprinkled from an evil conscience and our bodies washed with pure water. Let us hold fast the confession of our hope without wavering, for He who promised is faithful."* (Hebrews 10:16-23)

I know that's a long quotation, but I think it's a very powerful portion of scripture that many Christians gloss over, or don't fully recognize the importance of the author's statement. The veil has been removed by Christ and His blood. We know this, but do we *really* get it? We have a bold right to access the very holiest place, the Holy of Holies, the actual residence of Most High God; a new and living way to draw near unto Him with a true heart in full assurance of faith. What exactly are we entering into? What does it mean to "be in the Spirit"? Are these catchphrases we bandy back and forth, or do we genuinely believe we can experience the justice and mercy of God, one on one with Him in a private audience?

We have the means and the right—the imperative prodding of the Lord, no less—to enter into heaven's order here on this earth! We are expected to establish the order of righteousness where we are at. It is this loving-kindness founded on His justice that sees a person healed. This is one reason why children of God do not see their healing manifested. They do not understand the positional right they have under God's throne. Panoramic operation, initiating an encounter with God's rightness, helps to establish this truth in their life.

> *"For whom He foreknew, He also predestined to be conformed to the image of His Son, that He might be the firstborn among many brethren."* (Romans 8:29)

Christ is the firstborn of many. We know this. But what does that mean to be conformed to His image? It means we reflect His actual character; there is a distinct family resemblance to the way Christ operated on this earth. It's not just the forgiveness of sins and the new birth (of course those are the most important, don't misconstrue my intent)—but it is *also* His actions being duplicated and replicated exactly as He would do them should He be standing in our place at that very moment. Being conformed to His image is the point of this entire book you're reading. We have to be made to learn that it is our right and privilege, no—our *duty* to be fashioned faithfully, unerringly, after our Model, the first of many sons.

> *"But as many as received Him, to them He gave the right to become children of God, to those who believe in His name..."* (John 1:12)

The right. The power. To become children of God, not servants and slaves, not outcasts and aliens, not sojourners or illegitimate offspring. It is our authority given to us by believing in His name to be born again as children. True children, loved children, are highly prized, the greatest treasure any person can have. I think I've mentioned this before, but I've heard it said that in olden days the word for "child" and "wealth" were synonymous. This is who we are in Christ. Not who we *will* be, but in the present tense.

> *"For as many as are led by the Spirit of God, these are sons of God. For you did not receive the spirit of bondage again to fear, but you received the Spirit of adoption by whom we cry out, 'Abba, Father.' The Spirit Himself bears witness with our spirit that we are children of God, and if children, then heirs—heirs of God and joint heirs with Christ, if indeed we suffer with Him, that we may also be glorified together."* (Romans 8:14-17)

See the key there? As many as are led by the Spirit. That's what the Spirit is trying to do: bring as many sons and daughters into being as possible. Read Verses 1-9 of that same chapter for what it means to walk according to the Spirit. This book is trying to show some solutions for being led by the Spirit: panorama is one such way. Just two verses later (Verse 19) we are told that all creation eagerly awaits the manifestation of the sons of God. Why? Because we have the right and authority to perform the very same activities that Jesus did. We are joint heirs. And as such, we are expected, commanded, to operate in like manner. It is not an option. And if we are not performing those same acts (as a corporate Body and individually at least on some level, in whatever mode the Lord has commissioned us), we are failing in our capacity as a child of God. It's *that* important to understand this sonship anointing!

And why are we to operate as sons and daughters? To establish justice and mercy—the very foundation of the throne of the Father we worship.

> *"I beseech you therefore, brethren, by the mercies of God, that you present your bodies a living sacrifice, holy, acceptable to God, which is your reasonable service. And do not be conformed to this world, but be transformed by the renewing of your mind, that you may prove what is that good and acceptable and perfect will of God."* (Romans 12:1-2)

> *"...and be renewed in the spirit of your mind..."* (Ephesians 4:23)

To be transformed is to let the actual light of heaven be seen by others coming out through your renewed mind. Your face would glow, too, and you would know your right and authority over the enemy. There would be no unbelief. Now, before everyone gets all in a lather over this, that I'm being too "dominion" oriented and smacking of saying we should be glorified like Christ, keep in mind the entire context of this book, the crushings, the humblings, the joy of humility and repentance, the servant's heart. It is all of this (brokenness) that permits all of that (transformation.) It is only through Christ and in Christ that we have any kind of right and authority to act as Christ, to imitate His actions. Keep this teaching on sonship balanced with the teaching on humbleness.

But it is not either or, it is both!

> *"Beloved, now we are children of God; and it has not yet been revealed what we shall be, but we know that when He is revealed, we shall be like Him, for we shall see Him as He is."* (1 John 3:2)

"Now" in the above verse means, "right now." We're not sure what we *shall* be, but we know when that's revealed, we'll be like

Christ, for we'll see Him as He is *then*. But *now* we are children of God. This should create boldness in our lives (not rashness—they're two different things). Why are the sons and daughters of God so bold? Because they *know* the Father. They know He is the head of the house. They have no fear because heirs don't fear slaves—they are superior to them. You know what "overcome" means? You have come into a realm that is over. Over and above. Enhanced, outstanding, higher. We need to do away with this groveling slave mentality!

The children of God are full of courage because they know their place, and they know their Father has high expectations and hope for their futures. They are inheritors of that bright future based upon the foundation that was laid by the Firstborn. They have the full provisions of the Father's house. The keys to the larder, as it were.

In the Spirit, the sons and the daughters have authority. Authority is power, the right to act on another's behalf—in this case, on the behalf of the Lord Himself. How would He handle any given situation? I know right now you're probably looking for that old WWJD? bracelet, huh?

Power comes through sonship. Divine enablement comes with the calling of being a child of God. We possess the right or position in His house to exercise authority to release His power. It is delegated to us. That's an awesome responsibility! But even then, He is there to help us with that calling.

> *"In the day when I cried out, You answered me, and made me bold with strength in my soul."* (Psalm 138:3)

Read Zechariah 4:1-7. By His spirit, we cry grace, grace! And the Father responds. As we worship Him, as we cry out to Him, His loving-kindness and truth are released. This is the time you should read Psalm 8! Go ahead. I'll wait for you.

Back? Okay. Where were we? Oh, yes... it's a holy alliance with the Father. We as sons and daughters are bonded to Him, yet free. The children of His house go forth into the world, and the Father will glorify Himself in His children. That's the sonship anointing. Understanding this principle is important to earning the applause of heaven. They don't clap for servants, they clap for sons (and daughters... I tire of having to write this each time. You know what I mean, it's not gender specific.) Experiencing a true manifestation of panoramic activity is under-girded by being *au fait* (that's French!) with this concept of the sonship anointing. Some of the greatest miracles I've ever seen have come about from people just simply knowing this revelation of their sonship status in Christ.

But let's tie this into the flow of love as well. The sons express love to others without fear because they have a sense of their own self-worth. They can love the unlovely with no fear of being entangled by them, for they know their place in His house. The dirt of a sin-filled lifestyle has no appeal to them; yet they can reach down into the vilest pit to pull up one of the unwashed masses without fear of getting their own tunics dirty. The Father has broken the alienation that the people suffered under prior to being made sons. He has bonded them to Himself. They are *joined* to His Person.

> *"But he who is joined to the Lord is one spirit with Him."* (1 Corinthians 6:17) *"For through Him we both have access by one Spirit to the Father."* (Ephesians 2:18) *"...in whom we have boldness and access with confidence through faith in Him."* (Ephesians 3:12)

This sonship anointing brings unity with others in the same Body. You know, it's possible for us to reach a point together in the Lord that we can actually rejoice in the anointing of others, instead of being jealous for it! No longer isolated and afraid, the sons of God now enter into ministry with other people, to be witnesses together that touch empty, lonely hearts terrified of connecting with someone else's. They minister to the wanderers, the lawless, the aloof and discarded, the nomads.

In the Spirit, the sons have sound judgment. Discernment. What we've discussed ad infinitum (that's Latin!) in the course of this book. Because of that judgment, the sons are without fear of failure—they know they are pursuing the correct route in bringing forth the kingdom to others. They're not being led astray by wonky doctrine, strange spirits, foolish, fleshly activity.

They stand in the discipline of faith, confident they will make sound decisions, choosing the will of the Father in each instance, and thus, God will open up the heavens to them!

In the Old Testament, Moses illustrated what could be the norm in the New Testament. He showed what it meant to be a "friend of God" (see Exodus 33:11). To have that intimate communication where one speaks face to face with the Father. Notice in Deuteronomy 4:9-16 that the Israelites only heard the voice of the Lord, they did not see His form. Why is that? Because they would be tempted to make a replica of God's form and worship it as idolatry. God could only reveal Himself to the extent that they would not worship a substitute of Him. "I won't let you see My form," it's as if He told them, "cause you'll make it an idol, an image." And God won't share His glory with anything, even an image of Himself! It's either the real deal, or nothing at all. They would have worshiped the symbol, and not the Person it pointed to. Therefore, He did not reveal His form to the Israelites.

But not so with Moses! "I speak with him face to face, even plainly, and not in dark sayings; and he sees the form of the Lord..." (Numbers 12:8). God revealed Himself to Moses, face to face, mouth to mouth, eye to eye, so to speak. "...Hear now My words: if there is a prophet among you, I, the Lord, make Myself known to him in a vision; I speak to him in a dream" (Numbers 12:6).

Moses was the prototype of these "throne room encounters" we are supposed to have. They spoke together, friend to friend. Moses saw the Lord! But why? Here's the principle: to the degree that idolatry is removed from us is the degree that the Lord will reveal Himself to us. As strongholds are removed, it is our heart that sets the standard in what we see and experience.

God has already made Himself available to you; He hasn't moved. But His form is only revealed as you establish what is right in your walk with Him. It's simple, but intense. Study Hebrews 12:18-29. Remove anything that shakes, so that which stands firm comes to the forefront. The applause of heaven is given to those who understand their right and authority as a child of God to see their Father's form. By pressing in, drawing nigh, the sons of God can develop their spiritual faculties to such a point that the very Person of God is revealed to them. This revelation can be translated into their ministry operations, of which panorama is one facet. Therefore, come forward, sons of God!

THE DOWNLOAD
OF FAITH

FAITH, AS I'VE SAID MORE than once or twice in this book, is a significant factor in panoramic operation. And like I mentioned earlier, not just *our* faith, but a gift of faith from the Father. Specifically for panorama: His faith is downloaded into our lives to see the completion of the healing miracle. Without it, I am convinced, the greatest manifestations of His glory are thwarted, simply because we cannot believe to the same degree He can concerning those types of miracles. So let's take a bit and talk about this downloaded faith. Sound good?

In the miracle ministry of the seer, moving in panoramic operation for the discerning of spirits, the gift of faith (see 1 Corinthians 12:9) as we mean it, is a manifestation of God's faith in Himself to serve as a catalyst to experience the sovereign, supernatural intervention of the Lord. This is not the only expression of the gift of faith, but for the purposes of our study, this is the definition we mean. "Therefore I say to you, whatever things you ask when you pray, believe that you receive them, and you will have them" (Mark 11:24). This is a promise to have God's faith mixed with our own. It is a promise to a higher order of life by operating in a higher order of faith than what is normally available to us as sons of God.

It is a faith that gives us victory in battle. "And so it was, when Moses held up his hand, that Israel prevailed; and when he let down his hand, Amalek prevailed" (Exodus 17:11). A faith that meets domestic material needs (see 2 Kings 4:1-7). A faith for raising the dead. (see John 11). A faith for casting out demons (see Matthew 17). A faith for supernatural sustenance in famine and fasting (see 1 Kings 17). A faith for administering correction (see 2 Kings 2:23-24 and Acts 5). It's *this* kind of faith we are talking about here.

A downloaded gift of faith is the faith of the Lord turned back to Himself for receiving the astounding promises of God that in ourselves we have no means of believing for. The gift of faith is employed in securing the direct supernatural blessings that fulfill our own human utterances. Think about what that sentence means. It is what we decree that is backed up by God's faith. That's a lot of power to wield. Think of how this is incorporated in the healing anointing, specifically when mixed with the prophetic seer operation and moving in panorama.

"You will also declare a thing, and it will be established for you; so light will shine on your ways." (Job 22:28)

The gift of faith is an impartation of the Holy Spirit directly and supernaturally into the believer. As such, there is no cultivating this kind of gift—it is given, or it is not, as each situation comes up. Simply put, a supernatural kind of faith is given only for a specific situation to meet a specific need. Once that need is met, the gift of faith lifts off.

A good example is Luke 8:22-25 when the Lord is sleeping in the boat that is being swamped by water; He stands and rebukes

the storm. At a moment of need, Jesus received a special impartation of God's own faith, and note: then a *word was spoken* to release
that faith. I am convinced the disciples could have done it; they
could have released that gift of faith and calmed the storm, but they
failed to exercise the right kind of faith.

At a moment of dire need, they opened their hearts to fear. But
the Lord, at the same moment of need, opened His heart to faith.
And that is why He asked them where their faith was. I believe
Jesus knew the disciples could not have had faith within themselves to speak to a raging storm and command it to quiet. He was
teaching them how they should tap into the Father's faith. Another
good object lesson is found in Matthew 14:25-33, Peter walking on
the water.

When the gift of faith is in operation, a person—for that
moment in time—becomes the channel of God's own faith. It's not
so much the person who speaks the word that is so important, but
the faith behind what is being spoken. Our words can become just
as creative as God's when they are backed by His faith.

> *"By the word of the Lord the heavens were made, and all
> the host of them by the breath of His mouth. He gathers
> the waters of the sea together as a heap; He lays up the
> deep in storehouses. Let all the earth fear the Lord; let all
> the inhabitants of the world stand in awe of Him. For He
> spoke, and it was done; He commanded, and it stood fast."*
> (Psalm 33:6-9)

Our prayers can become channels for His faith to flow through—
a brief command energized by supernatural faith. "And the prayer
of faith will save the sick, and the Lord will raise him up. And if
he has committed sins, he will be forgiven" (James 5:15). A good
example is the raising Lazarus (see John 11:43). In the account of
Elijah declaring no rain to Ahab, we find the proclamation was

according to "my word" (1 Kings 17:1). See, there was a joining of Elijah's word with that of the Lord's—faith the fruit releases faith the gift! God backed up Elijah according to *his* declaration.

Those who possess the gift of faith believe God in such a way that He honors their word as His own and miraculously brings it to pass! A good illustration to consider would be those higher-order deliverances, the kind Jesus said only come out with "prayer and fasting" (Mark 9:29). This concept sort of ties into the Sonship Anointing we talked about earlier—our positional authority grants us the right to speak as the Father would speak.

This is part of the great power and great grace Acts 4:33 is talking about. But don't forget, though, that God still retains the initiative in bestowing a gift of faith—it is as the Spirit wills that the specific need is met with His kind of faith (see 1 Corinthians 12:11). This is why discernment is so vital—to follow the promptings and inner witness of the Spirit to avoid presumption! Remember, Jesus didn't curse *every* fig tree that had only leaves (see Matthew 21:19). We must learn to be reverent and careful, not expecting the world to jump at every little command we utter.

Because it is God's faith, and He retains the right to it, only lending it out as He wills, we are wise to remember that when the need is met, He withdraws His faith. We are then left once again with our own measure of faith that is to be exercised and grown as a grain of mustard seed (see Matthew 17:20). We're talking more about quality here, than quantity.

This gift of faith is a different impartation of a grace expression from workings of miracles. I believe creative miracles require a gift of faith, but workings of miracles is a gift we can receive as well. Workings of miracles *does* things by the Spirit, whereas faith's power receives or *enjoys* things by the Spirit. Workings of miracles is more active; the gift of faith is more passive. The gift of faith comes from the Spirit so that one might *receive* miracles, rather than *work* miracles.

While it is a great thing to covet spiritual gifts, including the gift of faith as needed… remember that there are preordained "glory encounters" that will take the gift of faith to enter into, and these glory encounters come many times in the midst of great adversity. It is the dire circumstances that generally demand an intervention of God's faith in the mix to solve the problem.

Further, the gift of faith employs *active* faith that *passively* expects a miracle. That sounds odd, but ponder that sentence for a few seconds. This is the case of a sustaining or continuous miracle. A miracle that is working secretly, silently over long periods of time, giving present assurance of future certainties, invisible realities. For a great testimony on this, may I suggest my son's and daughter-in-law's booklet, *Eight Weeks with No Water*, on how my grandson, Christian, was miraculously sustained over a four month period of time, two months of which he was in the womb with no amniotic fluid. A fantastic biblical example is Daniel's deliverance from the lion's den (a workings of miracles) while his protection was a sustaining gift of faith (see Daniel 6).

> *"By faith Isaac blessed Jacob and Esau concerning things to come."* (Hebrews 11:20; see also Genesis 27)

Now this gift of faith in panoramic operation ties into the "rest" that we are supposed to enter into. Because it is God's faith working, there should be an element of relaxation, respite, in seeing the miraculous healing anointing work. "And He said, 'My Presence will go with you, and I will give you rest'" (Exodus 33:14).

What does that mean, rest? A marked absence of stress, conflict, turmoil, tension and hassle. Rest in the midst of activity—the rest of faith: a place of rest where faith functions at top facility. "There remains therefore a rest for the people of God" (Hebrews 4:9).

Rest, as we mean it in the gift of faith and the release of panorama, is the ability to function at full capacity and strength, all the while being sustained by an inner-working, an "in-strengthening."

This kind of rest ties into our faith to live by—which is different than a gift of faith—that general attitude we have of trust toward God. "But without faith it is impossible to please Him, for he who comes to God must believe that He is, and that He is a rewarder of those who diligently seek Him" (Hebrews 11:6). This kind of faith is what motivates, directs and enables us to continue in a personal relationship with God; it is the grounds for righteous living.

It is supposed to be developed, which is where faith the fruit comes into play, leading into rest in the release of a gift of faith when needed. Faith the fruit is the essential nature of belief that always agrees with the definition of faith presented by Hebrews 11:1; "Now faith is the substance of things hoped for, the evidence of things not seen." Faith the fruit is the foundation for faith the gift.

Now, look, all faith is God's faith, okay? No matter what we term it. But the sovereign, supernatural manifestation of a gift of faith is of a higher order, a special thing originating from God, an actual aspect of His own eternal nature being revealed; and therefore there is no limit to this kind of faith. But let us never forget it must be God's own faith imparted directly by the Holy Spirit into us as believers at a moment of need. And then, remember a word is spoken to release the faith—a brief command energized by the supernatural faith. The gift of faith often serves as the catalyst to bring the other gifts of the Spirit into operation. Couple this with the seer operation in expressing a healing anointing, and we get a well-rounded, panoramic release of God's power to meet the needs; and by His grace and faith, we'll hear the clapping of those who have gone before us in heaven.

USSR

I N THE SPRING OF 1991, we were invited on a ministry trip to Russia right before the attempted coup d'état in August that led to the dissolution of the Soviet Republic on Christmas Day. This trip was a very rare thing, because just a few ministers were permitted visas into the Soviet Union at the time. After ministering in Russia, we slipped west from Moscow into the Latvian capital, Riga, and then into a town twenty-some miles southwest called Jelgava (Google it for the pronunciation). A Bible school had been established there just a couple of months earlier, out of Calvary Ministries International, and, if I'm not mistaken, was the first truly charismatic Bible college founded in the former USSR.

The director had been a little discouraged, because even though they'd sent out adverts, there was very little response, and the school consisted of him and his family, an interpreter, and just a couple students. They had been thinking perhaps they'd missed God's will and were considering shutting the college down.

One morning, while he was praying, he felt impressed by the Lord to go to the train depot. Thinking it strange, he nevertheless went to the depot in obedience to the inner leading. Once there, looking around, he spied a husband and wife, with a couple of kids and large suitcases, seeming to be displaced as if they didn't know where to go. So following the nudging of the Spirit, he approached them and asked if there was anything he could do to help them and why were they here, looking lost.

The wife spoke better English than the husband and told the director something to the extent of, "You won't believe this, sir, but my husband was a very wealthy businessman and landowner. We both had a dream from the Lord that told us to sell off what we owned and come here to Jelgava. God told us to stand at the depot until His man came to meet us, who would help equip us for the work of the ministry. You probably find this strange, no?"

The director recovered from his shock and said, "Well no, 'cause I'm the man. Come with me."

Over the course of the next few weeks, sometimes two or three times a day, the director went to the bus depot, the train depot, sometimes into Riga for people who flew in, and would collect those who had been told to come to Jelgava for ministry training by dreams, or visitations from the Lord, or by prophetic words. I believe the number was 178, from everywhere in the surrounding Soviet satellite states, the firstfruits of this Bible college.

They'd been in session, I think, three weeks when we got there. I taught with the aid of a wonderful interpreter, and when I was finished I felt the Spirit of the Lord fall on me. I realized it was an unusual anointing, very deep, weightier, heavier. I knew it was a special time of prophetic ministry.

I called a couple up and began to prophesy over them. About a third of the way through, the interpreter stopped me and said, "What are you doing?"

"Uh, giving them a word of the Lord."

"What do you mean?"

It dawned on me, they'd only been in session a few weeks and hadn't had time to get to personal prophecy. They'd never heard of it before, so I had to back up and give a little teaching on it. Once the foundation was laid, they received the ministry very well. The words, in my opinion, were incredibly specific—it was awesome to be a part of that. As I spoke in a *nabiy'* flow, I would look above their heads and see a ticker tape of their destinies, callings and giftings.

Even though the ticker tape was coming to me in English, I couldn't pronounce the names of the cities, some new, some home-towns, I was seeing that these people were supposed to go into, so I'd spell them out and the translator would go, "Oh, you mean, Blagagdaflagritzbonanana," or wherever. And I'd be like, "Yeah, that's the place..." The Lord revealed what the names of their churches would be, who some of their elders should be, people with first names like Igor and Boris and Vladimir. It was fun and astounding!

They'd never seen anyone slain or intoxicated in the Spirit before. The works were so deep, some would lay there an hour, two hours, three hours. Healings and deliverances were released with the prophetic mix.

Those 178 people became the foundations for most of the churches, intercessory groups and traveling ministries in their respective areas of influence.

One man, I recall, stood before me, and the panorama showed he had given up the greatest thing in his life for the ministry.

I said, "I see you on a platform singing to thousands of people, and you laid your guitar on the stage, surrendering it to the Lord. He says because you did that for Him, there will come a time that you will pick that instrument back up and go into the country of..." I stopped because what I saw was ROMANIA. And I thought, *That's, like, a thousand miles from here, isn't it?* Not a quick trip around the block, you know? But it was so specific, I just took a step of faith—which is always a key to panoramic operation, believing the Lord is trustworthy to add His faith to yours.

"Well, okay, I see you going back into Romania, and your praise and worship will be used to sweep thousands of youth into the kingdom of God."

The man shook and fell out under the power of the Spirit, where he lay for an hour and half. When he came to, he staggered up to me, intoxicated in the Lord, and asked if anyone had told me who he was. Boy, if I've heard that once, I've heard it a thousand times. I assured him I had no idea who he was.

"Six months ago I was the number one rock singer in Romania. In the middle of a rock concert with twenty-two thousand young people, I was convicted by the Holy Spirit, remembering when my mother,"—it might have been his grandmother—,"used to sit me on her knee and tell me about salvation in Jesus. I stopped in the middle of a song and fell on my knees and got saved—people wondered what was wrong with me. I was instantly baptized in the Spirit.

"I laid my guitar down on the stage and told everyone I gave it up for the Lord, and if there was anyone else who wanted to give their life to Jesus, come on up. Two thousand people came forward to get saved. After, I had a supernatural visitation that told me to come to this Bible college."

When he'd graduated from the school, God began to give him songs, and I was told he became one of the premier praise and worship leaders in the European Theater, producing many albums and DVD symposiums on worship.

What a remarkable experience to be a part of!

INHERITING A REVIVAL

A s we draw this book to a close, we've one last item to discuss in what I felt the Lord show me were keys to experiencing the applause of heaven. That is *inheritance*. While I am convinced that humbleness and brokenness are the greatest factors in seeing a greater expression of God's power released, we cannot forget the importance of compassion, faith, and righteousness. We've discussed panorama quite a bit, how the seer operation should be intertwined with the release of the healing anointing, the magnitude of developing a discerning spirit, and we've shared some testimonies that I hope will encourage your faith to press into that secret place with the Lord and find your own expression of ministry that completes the body of Christ.

If we were to sum up all of these items above, it can easily be encapsulated in the word *revival*. I am a revivalist—I love to see people in churches get set on fire for the glory of the Lord. The longer I've been in ministry, the more I've come to realize that revival is supposed to turn into vitality, leaving off the "re-" part, so we just have "-vival." (So not a real word, but it conveys the thought.) A way of life that expresses the fullness of everything Jesus wants His Bride to do in His name: all the signs, wonders, miracles, mighty deeds, deliverances, healings, salvations—the life of the kingdom, here and now.

Before we can get to that as a way of life, we must prepare for the next move of God. My definition of inheritance is probably a little different than you're used to. Most of us think, inheritance: taking up the mantle of the people who've gone before us, redigging the spiritual wells of old moves of God, somehow tapping into what happened *then* and bring it forward to *now*. Of course there's a correct notion in all of this. We are ignorant if we ignore (ignore/ignorant, see the connection?) of the mighty moves God did in the past. We should study our history and know it, live it, teach it. But perhaps I'm a bit more progressive in my perception of inheritance.

> *"When the Lord brought back the captivity of Zion, we were like those who dream. Then our mouth was filled with laughter, and our tongue with singing. Then they said among the nations, 'The Lord has done great things for them.' The Lord has done great things for us, and we are glad. Bring back our captivity, O Lord, as the streams in the South. Those who sow in tears shall reap in joy. He who continually goes forth weeping, bearing seed for sowing, shall doubtless come again with rejoicing, bringing his sheaves with him."* (Psalm 126:1-6)

What's really going to change our nation, our cities, our neighborhoods is preparing an inheritance for them to receive. The whole thrust of the kingdom is to bring that which was dead back to life once again, hence "revive." That's awesome! But the point I want to convey here is to *keep* it alive once it's been revived, otherwise God has to keep re-raising the dead over and over again.

Like the Israelites in the psalm above, we need the Lord to turn our captivity; yes, to revive us once again: so that He restores what was destroyed by the swarming, crawling, consuming, chewing locusts (see Joel 2:25). But we're to be revived so that we can give an inheritance to others. I am speaking about a sowing in your life that reaps a harvest in another's. Your being brought back to life, so that is translated into a testimony to bring others back to life.

You're supposed to be revived in your life so that it spills out to others. Revival, in my eyes, is not to be some exceptional moment Christians experience every once in awhile. It's supposed to be a way of life; it's "normal." Normal should be God in expression, glory, weightiness, power, signs, wonders, miracles as a regular occurrence.

"Of the increase of His government and peace there will be no end..." (Isaiah 9:7). God is always progressive in His purposes and movements, moving from "glory to glory" (2 Corinthians 3:18). It is a tragic mistake when the next generation works to preserve the "last movement." And often, God is forging ahead. What started in 1948 as the Latter Rain became the Charismatic renewal of 1965-67, which became the Jesus Movement of 1971-75, leading to the prophetic restoration of 1988 and then the apostolic re-establishment in 1997.

Of course we should appreciate what God did in the past. But I cringe when I see the body of Christ building monuments to the way things "were done." Looking backward continually stems from being a little afraid, or perhaps a touch lazy—it's a group of people, for whatever reason, who are unwilling to press forward into the way God wants things done now. So we see a dealing down of the power of the gospel to make it easier to swallow for the masses— this so-called Seeker-Sensitive Movement. It's not that everything about it is "evil" or wrong; it's just incomplete. And it has a tendency to create clueless Christians who have never experienced the power of God in the way He intended. They're dumbed down to a level of mediocrity that is rewarded by stagnation, and we wonder why society at large questions the relevancy of Christianity today! We need deliverance from this "form of godliness" (2 Timothy 3:5).

God still forges ahead. But are we being left behind?

One of the main components of this whole apostolic movement is creating spiritual fathers, right? But I ask, are the fathers leaving an inheritance to the sons? The whole point of being a father is to leave enough wealth so his children start at a higher level than he did. Isn't that what is termed the "American Dream"? Our ceiling of experience in the things of God should be the floor of our children's experience. That's what I mean when I say we need to leave an inheritance of revival.

But sadly, for the most part, revivals have not been built upon for the next generation to experience an increase. Each event was a singular occurrence for the people there at that moment. So the kids have to reinvent the wheel and dig out an expression for themselves.

For those of us coming out of the Jesus Movement, how often have we seen our kids experience the same kind of mind-blowing miracles, signs and wonders that we did? I bet very few. And that's sad, because now we have a generation of Xers and Millennium babies who don't know what we mean when we say, "Remember the Latter Rain and the Voice of Healing? Remember the Word of Faith? Remember the restoration of the office of the prophet and apostle?" We get a sea of confused faces growing up in a "seeker-sensitive" church.

And, you know, where are the seekers? I don't see a whole lot of seeking. I see an awful lot of sitting.

Okay, so that's the gloomy news. What's the answer? When we sow in tears, we'll reap in joy. We must sow for the next generation with our tears. It's too long to copy here, but please do take a moment to study Mark 9:14-29. The father's tears created a platform for the son to start at a higher level. "I have unbelief. Help my unbelief." So the son didn't have to inherit his dad's unbelief, yet he could inherit his dad's brokenness. And the boy would be able to say, "I have faith...because of the experience of my miracle."

You inherit what you didn't earn. That is the nature of grace for miracles. Now, that's not to say you don't have to pay the price to *develop* what you got for free, especially for future impact, which is what we're talking about here. The gifts are free. Maturity is costly.

But I am convinced God never intended for what He was expressing to be diminished in the next generation. What was dealt with and put away is not supposed to be an issue for those coming after us. God does not want His kingdom advanced in this way. Stop, start, stop, start. Previous moves are to be perpetuated—we are not supposed to start over!

> *"When an unclean spirit goes out of a man, he goes through dry places, seeking rest; and finding none, he says, 'I will return to my house from which I came.' And when he comes, he finds it swept and put in order. Then he goes and takes with him seven other spirits more wicked than himself, and they enter and dwell there; and the last state of that man is worse than the first."* (Luke 11:24-26)

In the context of revival, the above passage takes on a poignant (can't believe that's a real word...) concept. When a place is occupied by a revivalist, a vacancy is created where the revivalist was before—from the previous move to the present move, you see? The enemy uses it as a platform to mock the move of God in the next generation (those who should be moving into the vacuum), and it's possible they're left off seven times worse.

We've been successful in occupying the truth of salvation, passing it on to the next generation. We've sort of been riding the wave of inherited faith for conversions. But as a general rule, has the gospel of the kingdom—the *real* gospel of the kingdom, with signs and wonders following it to prove its validity—been preached as it should? Boy, if all the generations leading up to this one could answer Yes to that question, imagine what we would be seeing now!

I believe the time is NOW. The kingdom of heaven is here. The restoration of authority and confidence is upon us. The war with our wilderness is coming to an end. The dross has come to the top. A refining process has begun, and we are now making sense of life-changes around us, transitions, that create an inheritance for our spiritual and natural sons and daughters. That's why this is a good book to read (chuckle, chuckle). It provides some "how-to's" on what's a good inheritance to give your children.

Let me share three phases we all go through when coming to the next chapter of our lives. It's real simple, but we often spin in circles, trying to figure out what's coming next, where is God off to now? It's not all that bewildering. We make it harder on ourselves to perceive the next move of God than it should be.

Step One: the next move of God starts when there's an end to the way things were done. A death, so to speak. That's the first part of this book: repentance, brokenness, humility, crushing.

And Step Two, yes, there's a period of confusion—it is part of the transition. It's okay to feel a little fish-out-of-water from time to time when we see God doing something new. When we experience Him in a way we've not experienced before, there is a *shock*. But I believe we're swiftly coming out of this, and our befuddled generation of next-ers are getting the picture.

Step Three, the new beginning, er... well, it begins. That's deep, isn't it? God starts something new, and it's up to us to keep it alive so He doesn't have to keep reviving it. Take what we've learned, what we've experienced, and convey it to the next generation, so they're not rubbing two sticks together out in the wilderness trying to create a spark. Hand them your burning torch!

But it's our minds and emotions that resist change—hence the crushings of the Spirit. Our minds are hostile toward God (see Romans 8:7). The junk we've developed in the last move resists the experiences God has in the new season. So how does He get rid of the junk? We go through involuntary circumstances that "kill" the previous seasons in our lives—see Step One.

And it's uncomfortable, but this is God prepping us for what's coming next. The key is to hold on to it, not lose its sharp-edge, translating it to the kiddos coming after us.

The keys to inheriting a revival? Be honest with God. I find that most people do not pour out their hearts to Him as much as they should. They don't cry out with tears as they should.

How do you cry out? Ah, this is so simple, it's almost always overlooked. Find your voice in the Psalms. There you will read your heart's cry. Live in them, weep over them. But lastly, and perhaps most importantly, one of the factors this whole book has been trying to show: wait for it. Wait for the peace to bring you into understanding—wait in silence, in rest, in the secret place before the Lord. There's a point where you're done crying, your eyes are red and swollen, and you're just... silent. That's the moment the captivity is turned.

We simply do not spend enough time on our knees, just worshiping Him. We badger Him with our needs, our worries, our wants—as if He is unaware of them or something. No, don't freak out now—I'm not saying there isn't a time for that in our communication with the Lord. Remember the bit above about the Psalms and tears and crying out?

But let's be honest with ourselves. Most of our prayers consist of petitions, right? Honey-do lists. That's different than weeping before the Lord for one more revival, this time so we can keep it alive as an inheritance to our children.

That's one thing *my* inheritance showed me. It's the worship of the Bride that gets the Groom's attention, not her complaints. The Golden Candlestick was *all about* worship. Yes, intercession as the Lord directed. But the majority of their time was spent simply loving on the King.

There's no room here to describe in detail our connection with Frances Metcalfe's covenant group, the Golden Candlestick, the rich inheritance we walked into. We compiled a book called *Ladies of Gold* that explains it all. That's not shameless plugging—it's one of those previous moves we're supposed to recover and translate to the kids. We're just now coming back to the stuff the ladies uncovered sixty years ago. That's okay. We won't lose it again!

So what's the answer? What do we do to turn the tide, so to speak? I don't ever want to write a book that presents nothing but questions. I want to find the answer. I want to experience the applause of heaven.

> "*The secret things belong to the Lord our God, but those things which are revealed belong to us and to our children forever, that we may do all the words of this law.*" (Deuteronomy 29:29)

It's the prophetic revelation that reveals our inheritance! Ah, we're back to square one. Can we see a powerful connection between the seer operation wedded to a healing anointing, bringing signs, wonders, miracles, all that good stuff of the kingdom, the wild, startle-you-awake aspects of panorama? What can we give our kids? A discerning heart to perceive the revealed things of God. So you're not so much developing a seeing eye, a hearing ear, a perceiving heart for yourself—but for those coming after you.

Redeem your captivity, and there will be those who've gone before us thundering in heaven with applause!

ABOUT THE AUTHOR

James Maloney has been in full-time ministry for nearly forty years. He is the president of The ACTS Group International, an apostolic vehicle for *Activating*, *Counseling* and *Training* in the *Supernatural*. It provides opportunities for equipping, imparting and mentoring to this generation of ministers, and the next, who are eager to see a fuller release of the miraculous power of Jesus Christ, by hosting groups in overseas crusades and national conferences.

His other books include *The Dancing Hand of God*, *The Wounded Cry* and the forthcoming series on Christian doctrine, *Aletheia Eleutheroo*. He is also the compiler for the three-volume *Ladies of Gold*, the collected writings of the Golden Candlestick.

James and his wife, Joy, live in the Dallas-Fort Worth area with their grown children and six grandsons.

For more information, please contact:

The ACTS Group International

P.O. Box 1166
Argyle, Texas 76226-1166

www.answeringthecry.com

IN THE RIGHT HANDS, THIS BOOK WILL CHANGE LIVES!

Most of the people who need this message will not be looking for this book. To change their lives, you need to put a copy of this book in their hands.

> But others (seeds) fell into good ground, and brought forth fruit, some a hundred-fold, some sixty-fold, some thirty-fold (Matthew 13:8).

Our ministry is constantly seeking methods to find the good ground, the people who need this anointed message to change their lives. Will you help us reach these people?

> Remember this—a farmer who plants only a few seeds will get a small crop. But the one who plants generously will get a generous crop (2 Corinthians 9:6).

EXTEND THIS MINISTRY BY SOWING
3 BOOKS, 5 BOOKS, 10 BOOKS, OR MORE TODAY,
AND BECOME A LIFE CHANGER!

Thank you,

Don Nori Sr., Founder
Destiny Image
Since 1982